NORTHERN APPALACHIA REVIEW

VOLUME 5

CATAMOUNT
PRESS

an imprint of Sunbury Press, Inc.
Mechanicsburg, PA USA

CATAMOUNT
PRESS

an imprint of Sunbury Press, Inc.
Mechanicsburg, PA USA

For information about special discounts for bulk purchases, please contact Sunbury Press Orders Dept. at (855) 338-8359 or orders@sunburypress.com.

To request one of our authors for speaking engagements or book signings, please contact Sunbury Press Publicity Dept. at publicity@sunburypress.com.

FIRST CATAMOUNT PRESS EDITION: February 2024

Set in Adobe Garamond.

Publisher's Cataloging-in-Publication Data
Names: PJ Piccirillo, et al.
Title: Northern Appalachia Review Volume 5.
Description: First trade paperback edition. | Mechanicsburg, PA : Catamount Press, 2024.
Summary: An academic literary journal focused on writers from the northern Appalachia region.
Identifiers: ISBN : 979-8-88819-180-4 (softcover) | ISBN : 979-8-88819-181-1 (ePub).
Subjects: FICTION / Anthologies | LITERARY COLLECTIONS / American / General | FICTION / Cultural Heritage | POETRY / American / General.

Designed in the USA
0 1 1 2 3 5 8 13 21 34 55

For the Love of Books!

Northern Appalachia Review

Editor-in-Chief and Founding Editor: PJ Piccirillo

Nonfiction Editor: Rita Wilson
Fiction Editor: Amanda Gipson
Poetry Editor: William Scott Hanna
*Editor, Book Reviews, Interviews, and Literature of the Outdoors and
    Environment:* Dominique Hoche
Copy Editor: Debra Reynolds
Managing Editor: Samantha Backstrom
Assistant Poetry Editor: Kathleen S. Burgess
Administrator: Nicole Ravas

Fiction Readers
Nicole Ravas
Debra Reynolds
Arthur Turfa
Samantha Backstrom

Poetry Readers
Kathleen S. Burgess
Matthew Vargo

Nonfiction Readers
Nicole Ravas
Debra Reynolds
Ben Moyer
Dani Lamorte

Cover Art: from iStockPhoto
Cover Designer: Lawrence Knorr
Book Designer: Crystal Devine

Advisory Board
Brad Barkley
Bonnie Culver
Gerry LaFemina
Nancy McKinley
David Poyer

The Northern Appalachia Review publishes once annually. U.S. subscription rate is $20 for one copy. See submissions guidelines at NorthernAppReview.com. Address all correspondence to The Editors, generalinquiries@NorthernAppReview.com.

CONTENTS

KEY:

F—Fiction
NF—Non-Fiction
BR—Book Review
P—Poetry

The World Comforter

She stood in front of the Tioga County farmhouse and folded her arms, letting her eyes trace the roofline dipping toward the centered chimney, the warped cedar shakes above the screened porch, and the Pennsylvania bluestone path leading from the front door to the gravel driveway.

Well . . . there is a certain charm about it. A fresh start could be good.

Her father had bought this farm two decades ago, just after her mother died. By then he'd retired from a successful career in cotton sales. Every crib blanket sold during the baby boom had been manufactured with his products.

She was concerned about him living alone in the country but her brother argued that it was their father's life to live. Her fears proved true when a rung collapsed on the ladder he climbed to scrape moss off the roof and he fell to his death. After the estate settled, her brother got the family's elegant colonial home in New Jersey that her sentimental father never sold. She inherited this weather-worn property in New York that bordered the Susquehanna River's final plunge into Pennsylvania.

The next year on a warm October afternoon she drove up with the last of her belongings, completing her move into the farmhouse. Her place in New Jersey needed some modifications before the sale was completed, and paired with the process of retiring, it delayed her arrival.

The drive up wove past maple and northern red oak trees glowing the color of bonfire embers against a brilliant cobalt sky. Nature punctuated an ending transforming to a beginning.

She emptied the car, carrying each box into the room where its contents would be used. A few hours later she paused for lunch, chewing mindlessly a bland ham and cheese sandwich purchased at the nearby truck stop. Every so often the silence would be broken by a loud pickup passing or Canada geese honking overhead enroute to the river.

The sun was just setting as she opened the last box in the kitchen and removed the newspaper-wrapped glassware. As she stacked them on a cupboard shelf, her hand brushed against a tagged key dangling from a hook inside the door. She held the tag out to read it.

"*Aha!* It's for the barn. Well now, let's go have a look."

When she unlocked the weighty padlock and slid aside the weathered doors, her first reaction was laughter. No Maserati gleamed inside. No treasure chest spilled rubies and diamonds, either. There wasn't even a hayloft or livestock stalls, as one might expect. Instead, she found what looked like the old oak desk that had been in her father's garment district office for decades.

Why is that here? Did Dad use this as an office?

She flicked the light switch. Beyond the old desk stood the treadle sewing machine that belonged to his mother. Her eyes lingered there for a few seconds, remembering him sewing cotton twill curtains on it for their kitchen. She smiled when she recalled the fabric's pattern—citrus slices in a vivid Mid Century Modern palette of orange, avocado, and mustard yellow.

Her eyes rose upward. She gasped when she noticed the massive metal shelves behind the machine. They extended the length of the barn and were stacked with bolts of fabric wrapped in plastic. In the center of the barn stood a long table marked with a grid pattern. An opened bolt of fabric lay atop it next to a large pair of dressmaker shears. She turned toward the far wall and saw a pegboard holding satin binding ribbon in pink, baby blue, mint green, and pale yellow. Alongside were spools of thread in matching colors. The palette reminded her of newborn babies, and when she further examined the fabric on the table, she realized it was the airy-woven cotton he had sold for crib blankets.

He'd reconstructed his former life in this barn.

She shook her head and then slowly smiled. *What on earth had he been up to?* Here sat his legacy, the fabric that made him a standout in the industry. However, this was the very fabric he couldn't sell once foreign textile mills dominated the market. These were the surplus goods that expedited his departure from his beloved profession. His greatest success, his ultimate downfall—this barn contained it all.

Something shiny next to the sewing machine caught her eye. It was satin binding attached to a baby blanket he'd been sewing with the treadle machine. It looked complete to her, yet the binding's thread was still tethered to the machine's needle. Her curiosity compelled her to fetch the shears and snip the threads, setting it free. The soft feel of the fabric as she brushed it first across her cheek and then cradled it in her arms brought a feeling of comfort that made her cry. She hugged it tighter as she imagined her father assembling it with loving precision.

A legal pad with the specifications for the blanket lay hidden underneath it on the sewing machine cabinet. She read the measurements and stitching details in his beautiful bank script. He hadn't written anything about the reason for creating the blanket. Was he sewing it for someone special? Filling an order? Proving to himself that he could do it alone?

It was an emotional moment. Memories surfaced of her father coming home late from work on the train from Manhattan and eating his re-warmed meatloaf dinner. She sometimes snuck downstairs to chat with him as he ate, but her mother would chase her away like a protective swan, flapping her arms and extending her long neck. "Get into bed *now*, young lady! It's past your bedtime."

On Saturdays her dad plodded through tasks her mother had compiled for him. Sundays he unleashed his playfulness and humor. Her brother hogged a good deal of his free time, though. They'd shoot hoops together on the driveway basketball court or toss footballs across the back lawn.

Usually, she and her dad got a few moments of quality time before supper. He'd listen empathetically to her stories of school bullies and answered myriad questions about his work. Her curiosity about cotton amused him, and he often brought home fabric sample books for her to play with.

Because of him she got her job with the craft store corporation. He knew everyone important connected to the industry. It didn't hurt that she graduated from NYU's business school, which of course he pulled some strings to get her into.

At that moment, she realized this barn also contained the legacy of the biggest influence on her life. She wouldn't have had her forty-year career if it hadn't been for all of this.

Before she fell asleep that first night in her new home, thoughts returned to the feeling of hugging that blanket and how comforting it had felt on an emotional day. She wondered what her father's plans were for the rest of that fabric. Did he plan to hire seamstresses and make more blankets using it all up? If so, what did he plan to do with the blankets? Sell them for profit? Donate them to the poor in America? Ship them abroad?

The answer came in her dreams: *Comfort the world.*

After breakfast the next morning, she returned to the barn and decided to cut a few lengths of fabric and ribbon to sew some blankets. She still had unpacking to do but had this gnawing sense that there was a looming deadline to get some of these made. By early afternoon, she had cut enough fabric and ribbon according to his specifications to assemble eight blankets—two in each color.

That was enough for now.

On her first sewing attempt the next day she had no problem edging the cotton fabric as he had specified. Attaching the satin ribbon binding proved nightmarish. It kept puckering weirdly and the corners looked lumpy.

What would Dad do?

She carefully removed the stitches and tried again. And then once more. On her fourth try, she got a result that was passable. This one she'd keep for herself.

* * *

It wasn't until mid-December that she completed the eight blankets. Eventually she had to buy a new sewing machine because thread kept snagging between the old treadle's bobbin and feed dog, eating up too much of it in the process.

At the local craft store where she bought her new machine, she came across white ribbon embroidered with words of encouragement in gold script: "Hope," "Strength," and "Love." She decided that she could sew a word into a corner on the backside, making the ribbon into a loop to fit over a thumb, like a security blanket. Of course, she tested out her concept on the first blanket she made, and the result was what she'd hoped. A few days later she returned to the store and bought out the ribbon.

By the beginning of 2020, she'd completed fifteen blankets. A rhythm was falling into place, and she looked forward to sewing serenity in the heated barn those dreary winter days. At January's end she had a pile of thirty completed.

She divided her week into cutting fabric and ribbon days, edging days, and binding days. Sundays were reserved for finishing them with the ribbon loops.

Most of what was going on in the rest of the world had escaped her notice. On the occasions she would listen to the news, one word kept getting repeated: COVID. It grew louder.

By February, people in Italy were in lockdown. She saw videos on TV of neighbors harmonizing from their balconies in Siena, singing in solidarity to comfort each other.

By March, she had a stack of sixty-five finished blankets wrapped in plastic bags. One for every year of her life, she thought.

What am I going to do with these blankets? Give them to senior living facilities? Veterans' homes? Nursery schools? I've got to do something with them. They should be out there bringing comfort to the world.

On March 14th, Tioga County reported its first COVID case and a state of emergency was called. In the days that followed, the state, the country, and the rest of the world shut down like falling dominoes. She was used to isolation, but knowing the world was cut off from her triggered anxiety. For the first time since she moved here, she felt trapped. Her cupboards were well stocked, something her mother had taught her, so food wasn't a concern. It was knowing that the small bit of human interaction she once had was now forbidden.

Comfort the world, her father said to her again in a dream.

How could she get these blankets to people?

She had never joined social media, but the pandemic forced her to open accounts on a couple of platforms to maintain some sort of interaction with humanity. In that process she came across a countywide group that tallied local cases (and the rumors about where they had been contracted).

In April, that group posted about a local man who was concerned about the pandemic's effect on the county's dairy farms. He had created a delivery service called The Happy Holstein, and through it, people could order groceries online. If you placed an order and paid on his website by Monday, he'd collect the goods from the farms on Friday and a mask-wearing employee would deliver the groceries to your front door on Saturday.

The idea appealed to her, so she ordered some brown eggs, cranberry goat cheese, creamy maple yogurt, whole milk, and a sourdough loaf made with locally milled einkorn flour. The quality was excellent, so she signed on as a regular customer. The Happy Holstein delivery drivers became her lone contact with the outside world. Quite often they'd arrive when she was doing yard work, so she'd chat with them from a distance on her lawn.

An idea occurred to her. She could tip her delivery person with a blanket, acknowledging the important service provided her with something to give the driver comfort. One Saturday in May she tucked a blanket inside a paper bag with a thank you note saying that this homemade gift was guaranteed COVID-free because she had had no interactions with others. Then she wrote across the bag, "To my grocery deliverer, with thanks," and placed it on the front steps.

She was in the barn sewing when the delivery arrived, so she missed the opportunity to explain in person. When she heard the driver's pickup pull away, she walked over to the front porch to see if her thank you gift had been taken. It was gone.

The following weeks she prepared a thank you package every Friday evening. Her biggest decision was which color blanket paired with which word of encouragement to give the driver. After a while that got tiresome, and she'd just grab the next blanket on the pile.

By June she was getting so fast at sewing these blankets that her total production number topped three hundred. Of course, she had kept track of every blanket made and the few she had given away. It wasn't on green ledger paper, though. Before the pandemic, she had bought a cloth-bound diary at the craft store. The citrus fruit pattern reminded her of her dad's curtains. This was where she intended to document fulfilling his wish. The first lengthy posts expressed her rolling emotions of the moment. Later her posts tallied just what she had created that day as well as the latest pandemic stats.

Sometimes at the end of a Sunday evening, she would sit with a glass of wine and muse over the progress of her work versus the rise in COVID. On one of those evenings, she checked her email and found a message from the young man who founded The Happy Holstein.

Hi,

One of my drivers got COVID and I had to fill in for him yesterday. My apologies for your delivery being so late.

She shrugged. It hadn't bothered her.

It was a rough day driving two routes covering opposite corners of the county. I was hungry, and when I saw your package, thought maybe it contained cookies, so I ripped it open in my car.

Inside was something I didn't even realize I needed.

Since I began this business, there have been just a handful of nights where I've gotten more than four hours of sleep. When I finally got home, I grabbed some food, and then took a nap with that blanket wrapped around me. I slept eight hours! That fabric is insanely soft and warm. When I woke up, I saw the word embroidered on the underside loop: strength.

Ma'am, I cannot tell you what it meant to read that.

That was the nicest thing anyone's done for me lately.

Brandon

P.S. Would you be interested in selling these?

She sat back from the computer. Her father's project may have found its direction. How many clients did Brandon have, and did she have enough product on hand if demand took off? What should she charge for them? Money was tight for everyone. Would that mean only people who could afford it would get them? Did that go against what her father intended?

Too many thoughts crossed her mind now to respond to him. She wanted to think through the logistics of setting this in motion, so she went to bed and hoped her father would provide an answer in her sleep.

She awoke with a full response to Brandon composed in her mind.

Hi, Brandon.

I'm so happy you enjoyed the blanket.

Your business model is great, and your exhausting work has helped so many in a time when the world needs it desperately. Thank you!

I have a limited inventory of blankets on hand. Can you give me a rough number of your customers?

A thought. How many drivers do you have? If the number is no more than ten, I could give you one for each driver every week and they in turn could give it away to a random customer.

There is no need for me to make a profit from these blankets. They are meant to bring people comfort. It's a long story that I'll share with you one day.

She signed her name, and then for some reason added *The World Comforter* before hitting send.

That afternoon when she'd finished sewing blankets for the day, she went back into the house and checked her email.

Dear "World Comforter," ;-)

Your kind offer impressed me. I am kicking around a few ideas for how the blankets could be distributed.

There are fifteen drivers on the team, including myself. You wouldn't have to give them each a blanket to distribute. Whatever number you determine is doable would be fine. Let me think about the logistics and get back to you.

She turned off the computer and went into the kitchen to make dinner. While she peeled potatoes in the sink she thought, *I'll start distributing them in this county. Once I get a feel for the demand, maybe I can send them elsewhere.*

Brandon responded Thursday.

Any chance you could have ten blankets ready for me to pick up tomorrow sometime?

She replied immediately.

Yes. I will bag them up and leave them by the front door.

That Saturday as she worked in the barn, she wondered whose homes the blankets were being delivered to and how their recipients reacted. Did they embrace them as soon as they opened the bags? She hoped so. It would be like getting a hug from her father.

Brandon emailed her at the end of the day with a list of recipients' addresses and a copy of the message he attached to each delivery:

Dear customer of The Happy Holstein,

You have been randomly selected to receive this free handmade blanket from The World Comforter, an anonymous seamstress living in our county. It's her desire to bring you comfort during this difficult time. This is made of 100% cotton and should be laundered gently. Guaranteed COVID-free.

Thank you for your continued support,

Brandon

She read his email the next morning, and then walked outside, pointed heavenward and grinned. "We did it, Dad."

It was a warm day in late June. She strolled joyfully down the path from the yard to the riverbed. The field lining the path hummed with crickets. Closer to the river red-winged blackbirds trilled from willow boughs, and honeybees danced over sweet peas and crown vetch blooming atop the bank. Something moved by the water as she neared. A great blue heron unfurled its massive wings and loped away overhead. She raised her hand to block the sun, squinting as she followed its slowly gliding path downriver. A large bass leapt and smacked the water, and she turned around to see it. That's when she noted a line of Eastern Painted Turtles sunning on a log in the feeder creek.

She closed her eyes as she stood on sun-warmed shale stones, pausing to hear the water's music as it burbled past to its rendezvous with Chesapeake Bay. This river had already brushed against cities and farmland as it flowed south from its source—the lake James Fenimore Cooper called Glimmerglass.

On her walk back to the house she noticed there were residents in the bluebird houses her father had erected. During her final visit with him here, he had proudly showed her the boxes made exactly to Audubon specifications. She hoped he'd gotten to see them being used.

Everything around her hummed with life, oblivious to the forced stillness upon the rest of the world. When was the last time in her life she'd felt such serenity? *No wonder Dad chose this place,* she thought.

* * *

With summer's arrival, people were able to gather socially distanced outside without fear of getting COVID. Experts determined the virus was airborne, so outdoor breezes dispersed it safely.

Brandon now spent time chatting with her when he stopped by to pick up the blankets. They'd sit kitty-corner from each other at the picnic table under the broad shade of the catalpa tree. Listening to him share his dreams, she couldn't help but be reminded of her father's work ethic. She told him about her dad's textile career and why he moved to this place.

Brandon recalled hearing about his death. Apparently, word spread fast across the county about his tragic passing. Seemed most people knew who he was. Waitresses at nearby Marlene's Diner said he had always tipped them well. Teachers at the local Head Start recalled how he grew mini pumpkins in his garden that he donated every Halloween to the kids. Brandon's uncle was a mail carrier, and this house was on his route. Her father had brought him back a big box of Jersey Shore taffy in thanks for holding his mail when he went on vacation. The uncle said he'd never tasted taffy that good.

"Wasn't he in his 90s?" he asked her. "I wonder why he didn't just call a neighbor for help with the roof instead of trying to do it himself. Though your dad was from New Jersey, he sure was as stubborn as a Tioga County farmer."

That made her laugh.

During their chats she gave Brandon business advice. Sometimes he'd give her groceries left over from the Saturday runs. The frequency with which he did that though made her suspect that it was his way to pay her back for the blankets, which had become a huge selling point.

"I hate to even ask this," he said one September afternoon. "Is there any chance I could order a blanket for my sister? She's an influencer, and I know she'd talk about it on social media. We're doing so well right now, delivering to three counties, that I'm thinking of expanding even farther east."

"What's an influencer?"

"She displays products on her social media accounts. Her posts get so much traffic that companies pay her to promote their goods. Earns a ton more than I do."

"Who knew you could get paid to do that? Smart concept. Little overhead."

"I've been after her to feature our products. She keeps saying she'll get around to it. One of your blankets might convince her. She's nearing a million followers around the world."

"Whoa, I couldn't boost my output to meet that sort of demand, Brandon. This consumes most of my time now and sewing twenty-five blankets a week is enough."

"Oh, no. I'm just thinking of the local followers. They might become customers if they think there's a chance of getting one of your blankets for free. You never know. Someone might even make me an offer for my business."

She smiled at his ambition, and then paused before speaking.

"Growth is good, Brandon. However, the very fact that you are not a corporation but instead a grassroots effort rising to meet a specific local need is one of your biggest selling points. Don't lose sight of that."

He thought about what she said and nodded.

"What color blanket and what word do you want sewn on the back?"

Brandon grinned. "A pink one, with the word 'love' sewn on it."

"I'll have it ready for next week's pickup."

* * *

Brandon's sister gave him a suspicious look when he handed her the shopping bag.

"What's this?"

"Each week, ten customers get one of these blankets for free with their groceries. I asked the seamstress if she'd make one for you because you're my favorite sister."

She lowered her eyes. "I'm your *only* sister." She peeked inside the bag. "Is this a baby blanket?"

"Technically, it's a crib blanket. It's big enough to wrap around an adult."

She raised her eyebrow. "That's a little weird."

"Take it out, feel it. You can't get a cotton blanket that soft anymore. It's made with vintage fabric from the Sixties. Plus, on the flip side there's a word to inspire you."

She pulled the blanket out and brushed it across her face.

"It *is* soft. And it's pink—my favorite color." She flipped over the blanket to find the word.

"Look in the corner there," he said, pointing.

Her eyes softened when she saw the message. "*Love?* That's what I end all my posts with: #Love."

"I know. It's perfect for you."

"So, when the orders are delivered each week, totally random people get free blankets?"

Brandon nodded.

"Could I buy one from her? Maybe one larger to fit my queen-size bed?"

"She's not selling these. It's something she's doing to fulfill her late father's wish."

"What other colors do these come in?"

"Mint green, baby blue, and pale yellow."

"I want them *all*. Can I get one in each color?"

"Don't be greedy, sis."

"OK, could she give you swatches of the other colors then?"

"I can check with her."

* * *

Brandon's sister posted about The Happy Holstein on her social media the next Friday. He was slightly annoyed that the free blanket got more mention than the farms his service represented or the wide variety of products they offered. Any advertising, though, was better than none.

The next day Brandon's email box brimmed with inquiries from potential customers. Also, a producer from a network news show asked him to call.

"Holy . . . ! She's got quite a reach." He looked at the clock. It was after five. "I wonder if this producer's still at work?"

His heart thumped as he dialed her number.

"Hi Tamika, this is Brandon, the owner of The Happy Holstein."

"Thanks for calling, Brandon. Our evening newscast has been interviewing local heroes throughout the pandemic for our series 'America Stands Together.' I saw a post on social media about your business and it sounded perfect for us. May I ask you a few questions?"

"Sure."

By the time Brandon hung up, Tamika had scheduled a video interview for next week. She gave him the name of the reporter and team who would be driving up from New York City. He was made aware of the various COVID protocols that had to be followed during the whole time the team was with him.

Brandon paced his kitchen pumping his fists into the air a few times, and then grabbed the phone.

"Hey Ms. World Comforter, you'll never guess what just happened."

She took such delight in hearing the news.

"Any chance we could stop by your barn and film, too?"

That thought gave her pause. *Would her father want this story exposed to the world, or would he prefer that the blankets be distributed quietly?*

"Let me get back to you on that. In the meantime, congratulations, Brandon. This is huge."

Inadvertently these blankets had just changed the fortune of a young man.

"Never doubt the power of cotton," she said to him, quoting her father's favorite truth.

* * *

The news team arrived late Thursday night to prepare for following Brandon's pickup runs the next day. Early Friday they began the day watching Holstein cows getting milked, then goat cheese being processed, and later interviewed a soap maker who used lanolin from her sheep's wool in her products. It was an exhausting day, but the team was so fascinated by the stories behind each product that they lingered longer than planned.

"Brandon, where are those blankets made? Can we meet that person?"

He had felt her reticence to being interviewed. She hadn't gotten back to him, but technically she hadn't refused to meet with them, either.

"It's my last stop of the day. She lives near me. Two more businesses before then."

* * *

He was later than usual getting to her house to pick up the blankets. When she saw two cars pull in the driveway, she frowned.

Oh no, what has he done?

He phoned her from outside and asked if she could put on a facemask and meet them by the barn.

Guess I have no choice.

She carried the blankets for Brandon out the back door. He introduced her to the news crew. They filmed her exchange with Brandon and asked if she could take a blanket out and show it to the camera. She turned it over when prompted so the cameraman could zoom in on the word of encouragement sewn onto the back ribbon—"Hope."

"Is this where the magic happens?" the reporter asked, pointing at the barn. She nodded. "Mind if we have a look." From the distraught look on her face, the reporter added, "Of course we'll socially distance once inside."

"I'm curious too," Brandon said. "I've never seen it."

I'm doing this to help Brandon's business, she thought as she slid the barn doors open and turned on the lights. The team filed in, keeping their distance from her.

"This is incredible. You did this all by yourself?" the reporter asked.

Before she could stop herself, she spilled her father's story, including every detail about his career, how fabric imports ruined it, and how he bought this farm after his wife died.

"He comes to me in my dreams sometimes," she said gazing at the wall of fabric, oblivious to the camera lens focusing on her face, "and he tells me to comfort the world. That's why I started making these to his specifications."

They spent hours talking about American business, foreign competition, rural life, and the interpersonal cost of the pandemic. She hadn't had such intellectual conversation since she left the corporation. Before they headed out, she went over to her stockpile of finished blankets and picked out one for each member of the news team.

Brandon waited until they pulled out of the driveway.

"Thank you for giving me the greatest day of my life."

"Pffft. I'm barely responsible for this, Brandon. Your hard work makes the story."

"Maybe, but these blankets are the hook. Everyone's going to be talking about this."

"When does it air?"

"Next Friday."

* * *

A week later she was sitting in front of the TV watching the evening news, waiting for the "America Stands Together" segment at the end of the broadcast. The video opened with a shot of her barn. It panned across the interior and then zoomed in on her, talking about her father giving her a message in her dreams to comfort the world.

"Uh-oh."

Soon it was apparent that *she*, not he, was their focus. The Happy Holstein was mentioned, and they did show video of Brandon at the farms picking up orders, but it was obvious that the story of the blankets intrigued the reporter most. The final shot was the reporter holding up a blanket and rubbing it gently against her cheek.

"You cannot believe how soft, how *comforting* this fabric is. Back to you, Gabriel."

"And that's how America Stands Together this week. See you Monday."

Her phone rang. She feared it was Brandon calling, angry at her for stealing the limelight.

Instead, it was her brother. Livid.

"What the hell are you doing? Why didn't you tell me about what was in the barn? I should get a percent of the value of that inventory."

"Oh, and it's lovely to speak with you, too. How much did you sell our home for? Five hundred thousand? Seven hundred thousand."

"No, I got a million five for it. It's a seller's market right now."

She hung up and then blocked his number on her phone.

Midday Saturday there was a knock at the front door from Brandon. Could they chat?

"Listen, I recorded the newscast and watched it later. I want you to know that I'm not angry. In fact, we have gotten many new customers since it aired, adding to the big increase we got from my sister's post.

"There's something else you need to see though."

He opened up a social media app on his phone. "Have you heard of that Italian model, Josefina? She's married to an NFL quarterback, and I just learned that she follows my sister's account. Today she posted this."

He handed her the phone so she could look at the image. Josefina pouted her unnaturally full lips as she snuggled a soft blanket against her makeup-contoured cheeks. The blanket looked just like the one she had made for Brandon's sister. Same color. Satin binding that matched. The next photo was a closeup of Josefina's thumb with a sparkling fingernail holding the blanket's loop that read "Love."

"Where'd she get my blanket? Did your sister send it to her?"

He shook his head and clicked a link below the photo. It opened an online storefront where you could buy Josefina's "COVID comforters" for $64.95. The product, she noted, was imported.

History had repeated itself, but this time with a twist.

"I'm so sorry," Brandon said. "Are you going to sue her?"

"Nah. I'm not trying to make money from these. My father stole this design from the blanket manufacturer. Whatever."

He scuffed his shoe at the ground. "So . . . will you still be sewing the blankets for us?"

"Of course."

* * *

The pandemic raged that winter, but she remained unscathed. In March of 2021, she booked a vaccine appointment as soon as they were available. Cases lessened as summer began and she felt confident to meet up with people from the online group who had also been vaccinated.

Some women expressed interest in learning how to make the blankets. They brought their sewing machines to the barn and set them up, socially distanced. Having those four women join in increased the output rapidly, and it was good because Brandon's business expanded north, east, and just across the border into Pennsylvania.

The number of fabric bolts stacked on the shelves dwindled. Some shelves had been emptied. They noticed that there were more bolts of yellow and green fabric left, so for a while they just sewed blankets in those shades.

On New Year's Eve, she was stunned to see the tally of how many they had completed: nearly seven thousand! How many would they finish in 2022?

The phone rang, startling her thoughts. It was her maternal aunt.

"Your brother has COVID and he's quite bad. On the respirator. No one can visit him in the hospital. Personally, I don't think he's long for this world. He told us not to contact you, but I think that's wrong. You're his sister."

"Oh no. Where did he get it?"

"Work."

"How are his wife and kids doing?"

"Dear, they got divorced not long after he sold your family home. He took up with some young thing. Lives in Manhattan. Can you believe it?"

Her brother died in January. No service. Nothing left to her. She wondered if his kids even got anything. He was never close to her, but she felt sad. He was the only living relative connected directly to her father.

Despite that, her father's presence remained here at the river's edge. Thanks to her sewing friends who dubbed themselves The Comforter Club, she was going to complete his wish.

One morning in July a car with Massachusetts plates pulled into her driveway.

Who's this? she wondered as she put on her mask to answer the door.

"I'm sorry to bother you, but are you the woman who was on that America Stands Together news story?"

"Yes. Why do you ask?"

"Thank you."

"Did you get a free blanket?"

"No. The thank you is actually meant for your late father."

That intrigued her. She stepped outside to chat on the front lawn, standing with her arms folded.

"You knew my father?"

"No. My name is Patrick Carroll. Your father and my dad knew each other."

"Was he in textile sales?"

"Actually, textile manufacturing. Cotton."

"My father sold his product?"

"Yes. It's what you have been using to make those blankets."

She covered her mouth with her hands.

"Dad was very proud of it." He looked toward the barn. "Is that where you work?"

She nodded. "Want to see it? Let me go get the key."

They walked inside past the half empty shelves and paused by a bolt of blue fabric. She pulled it off the shelf and set it on the table, sliding the fabric out of its bag. He touched it and then turned away. Was he crying?

"I'm sorry, has your father passed?"

He nodded.

"My father nearly lost the factory in the 1980s when imports took over the market. Teetered on bankruptcy. Then my mother died of breast cancer. Rough time."

"I'm so sorry."

"That's when your father showed up one day with a couple of tractor trailers and bought this fabric we couldn't sell. It saved our company. My father used that money to add poly-cotton blends to the product line and they were a success. The result was I was able to go to business school and eventually take over the company from Dad. He got to enjoy about ten years of retirement before he passed. I eventually sold the company. Just bought a lake house in Hammondsport. Thought I'd look you up on the way there. Always wondered where that fabric ended up."

"Are you hungry?" she asked. "I was just making some pasta salad. We could lunch out here at the picnic table."

"I'd hate to impose. . . ."

"Did I mention the strawberry rhubarb pie I bought at the Amish farm stand?"

He grinned. "What man in his right mind would refuse pie?"

Lunch stretched into dinner, followed over time by long phone conversations, dawn kayaking along the Susquehanna, dusk swimming in Keuka Lake.

* * *

On a sunny afternoon the next May, she fastened the barn door's padlock for the last time. The desk and sewing machine had already been moved to her new home in Hammondsport. Her friends in The Comforter Club had sewn a king-sized blanket with the last of the fabric and gave it to her and Patrick as a wedding gift. A metal recycler removed the shelves. The profit from that sale went to Brandon to expand his business.

She took a final stroll through the drifts of buttercups, past the bluebird houses, and along the shore to say proper farewell to the Susquehanna, and then headed back to where her husband awaited in the driveway. Her quickening stride flattened sedge and meadow grasses under foot, as her father's voice repeated in her mind: *Never. Doubt. The power. Of cotton.*

Sketchbook

This morning I tried again to sketch
the light on the holly tree.
To draw the density of slate-smooth bark,
the lake-deep eye of the mourning dove,
the gray catbird and her fuzzy mews.

I splurged on really good paper;
velum surfaced, toothy cotton pages
layered like skin, cavernous and marvelous
as cells under a microscope.

This morning I tried to dissect the sunshine
from the tree's edge.
I tried everything I knew—
scribbles, points, even hatching.

Attempts to blend the pencil with my finger
left the page blemished and bruised.
In desperation I shaded a fresh sheet
in graphite; cut out the holly
with a rubber eraser.

After all this time trying,
illumination is not something drawn,
but rather what remains
once the layers are lifted.

Appalachian Spring: A Morning Rhapsody

I slip out silently
into grayness.

Night chill lingers
in the morning dew.

World awakens with
stirrings on branch, in field.

Throats clear with
tentative chips and calls.

Alert, I watch . . . listen—

Spontaneous rhapsody
of light and melodies,

crescendo of radiance
and sound inexorably bound.

Birdsong at sunrise,
a fitting encomium

to this spring morning.

If I Am Allowed To Be Morning

On this hill country air, the smell of bacon
and coffee, the moldering walls of my trailer
porous as the skin of a leaf.
Tanager sings in and out of it.
Wood thrush settles down within it.
Towhee scuffs duff and stirs it.

After all my books are sold and
my cot is vacant with peace,
no more tossing, no more fumes
of the engine of dread
fouling the space above
where my sleepless head burns
as monkeys inside it leap and
scream.

Let me be morning, uncrowded.
Let me awake blank, fresh as the beginning
of any heaven's day
as it might be here on earth.

David M. Sweet

Persephone Returned

I remember well
your calico gown
stripped away from you—
replaced by those cold,
stark, hoary death shrouds.

And we wept, we mourned,
we longed for your breath
to form in darkness
under Orion—
wan moon looking on.

All at once, it seemed,
The Dawn Chorus burst
in symphony. Your
viridescent gown
laid among the hills.

Tress wreathed in dogwood,
hands brushing sarvis,
lips lined with redbuds,
you arose, saw me,
and opened my soul.

Locust

Locust blooms again
As if its days were not decades
Many times I have seen this
As if my decades were not days

All my loves live with me now
Birds sing all the music
I ever heard
Trees give me every green
There is to see

Air comes off the mountain
Like water
Touches my face, my skin
Lifts me
Holds me
Opens me

On the road
Young rabbit scurries away
With small bits of me

Just as each forsythia bloom
Drops parts of me
To fold into the earth

Each grass blade
Each photon of light
Each long sigh
Of the seasons

Erodes me
Like stones in the river,
Carries me to
Some where
Some thing
Some other

Each decade
Each day
Each hour

And yet,
There is still so much

How big I must have been
How big I will be

I go into the woods
Break locust blooms
Carry them home
For my bed

Fourth Month Full Moon

Fish moon, egg moon,
pink moon, sprouting grass moon.

I name this one:
spring peeper moon, tadpole moon,

moon that wants me awake
all night, wants more

light in my life, wants
to pull me upward

like crocus, daffodil,
wild onion, all the bulbs

that wait in soil
for the faintest touch.

Thirty-three years dead
yet beneath July peach trees
father gathers fruit.

Woven Lives

The clapboards on the mountain farmhouse had weathered to a soft gray. Blending into the faded color, barely visible smudges of a long-ago application of white paint outlined the casement windows. All the first-floor windows were open, curtains breathing in and out in a unison dance of spring. Lit by the sunrise peeking from across a partially plowed field, the forest on the ridge behind the farm shimmered with multiple shades of new leaves.

In the upstairs corner room facing east, Garrett McWhorter sat on the edge of his bed. Something was missing, lost. He tried to clear his mind. Had he forgotten to close a gate? Left the tractor still running in the field? He could hear sounds in the kitchen below. Hettie. No doubt fixing breakfast.

Other thoughts crowded into Garrett's mind. Why was he here in his father's old room and not in the larger bedroom he and Hettie shared? A vague memory surfaced, a discussion with his grandson Michael and Michael's father, Will. Something about the stairs, about the windows and the view of the barn and sloping pasture.

Garrett found his cane leaning against the nightstand. He scowled at the portable commode Michael had set up after the trip to Doc Adams. Three steps. He could do it. He rose from the bed, steadied himself with the cane. Not the stairs to the downstairs bathroom, not even with Michael's help. Not anymore. Knees wobbling, he backed up to the pot and pulled down his tattered long johns. He sat and let loose a weak stream. He groaned. Not natural for a man to sit and pee.

A soft knock. Had to be Molly.

He frowned and glared, tried not to sound cross. "Give me a minute. Please wait."

"I'll come back a little later, Gramp. Eggs or oatmeal, this morning? Or both?"

Molly, his grandson's wife, was lovely, patient. Garrett loved her as much as he loved Michael and the rest of his grandkids. But sometimes, just sometimes, it grated him she was so gol'durned nice. If she snapped at him when he was crotchety, he could understand it. God help him, he hated being so dependent.

Garrett managed to rise from the pot and stand without knocking the damn thing over. He cringed. Of course, it would have to be emptied. If Michael did it, he could stand it. But his wife?

When he and Michael had left old Doc Adams's office three weeks ago, a bag of medicines in hand, Michael had placed six phone calls and the decision was made. All Garrett's children agreed. Stay at home, if that's what Garrett wanted. Hire a nurse if it came to that. Follow the doctor's orders. Limited walking. No stairs. Garrett listened, agreed, and made the final decision: upstairs in the quiet comfort of his father's room viewing the pasture up to the fields and the barn he and his father had built so long ago. Molly had suggested a rented hospital bed in the parlor. Never. Hettie wouldn't stand for it. Moving out her grandmother's horsehair sofa, ruining the look of elegant comfort.

The last time Molly came in to get the pot, he had pretended to be asleep. Would she open the door while he struggled to pull up his underwear? Worse than Molly tending to his pot was if she'd see his aging privates flapping in the breeze.

From the other side of the closed door, Molly called out, "Gramp, what do you want for breakfast?"

"Oh, don't matter. Coffee, if there's any left." There, he'd said that nice enough.

"Of course. I'll bring coffee and eggs up in about ten minutes. Do you need help getting to the pot? Michael's gone to the barn, but he said he'd check back before taking out the tractor."

Christ! Damn pot again.

Garrett eased himself over to the rocking chair by the window. The trees along the edge of the pasture were greening out, and a sliver of the plowed field above shone dark and rich in the sunlight.

"Gramp, do you need Michael?"

"No, no, dear. I'm managing. Tell him to come up though."

* * *

Molly placed his plate of eggs, two biscuits, and his coffee on a metal tray with thin legs. A TV tray, she had said yesterday. Garrett didn't trust it. Flimsy. When Molly left, he sat forward in the rocking chair, his legs underneath the tray. He must not bump the damn thing. Molly was an angel. She hadn't said a word yesterday when his plate had rocketed off the tray onto the floor. In luck, he had held onto his coffee cup.

Garrett had finished his eggs and coffee when Michael came up the wooden stairs in his socks, his steps soundless.

"Another good day for plowing, Gramp. Feels good to be a little ahead this spring."

Garrett grunted and looked out the window. "I should be out there. That old tractor needs a firm hand, a smack with a wrench now and then."

Michael laughed. "That she does." He set Garrett's empty plate and cup on the desk and collapsed the tray to fit beside the bookshelf. "Want a different shirt today?" Michael pointed to the open closet door where Garrett's long-sleeved shirts hung, clean and ready.

"Yes," Garrett said. "Not the flannel. Something cooler." His hand shook as he pointed. "That red. Hettie likes it."

Michael took the shirt off the hanger. "Nana did like red."

After helping Garrett button his shirt, Michael took Garrett's overalls off the back of the desk chair and guided his feet into the legs. Garrett put his hands on his grandson's shoulders and stood while Michael pulled up the trousers and fastened the straps over the bib.

Garrett patted Michael on the back. "You're a blessing, boy. Hettie and me made a good decision having you and Molly move in. You milking? Susie still putting out four pails a day?"

"Best cow on this mountain. I milk in the morning, the calf takes his share, and Richard sends up his boy Butch in the evening. The Baileys appreciate the milk. We don't need six gallons a day now that Molly has all that butter and cheese in the freezer."

"What about Taffy? She jumping fences?"

Michael hesitated. "Nah, she's happy with the other horses. You remember. Dad has her with his three. Abby rode her up to Dad's place before she went away to school."

"Abby?"

"Your granddaughter. Abby."

Garrett sat in the rocker. He fingered the clasps on the overall straps. What had Michael said? Something about Abby. "Yes. Abby. She calls me. I remember. We followed in the Jeep. You and Molly had just moved in here."

Michael bent over and kissed Garrett on his forehead. "Four years ago. When Nana got sick again. We love being here, Gramp. Great place to raise our family."

Garrett grabbed Michael's hand. "You're so much like your dad. Of all our sons, Will was the best with horses. He taught Abby to ride, your brother Willy, and young Sarah. You, too, I guess."

"He sure did. Dad rides Taffy from time to time. Keeps them both fit. Taffy's fond of Mom's old, gray gelding. If the two-year-old goes after him, Taffy settles his hash quick. Dad says Taffy just wanted a herd, a family. She doesn't even think about jumping out."

When Garrett released his hand, Michael bent down to grab the plastic pot that had come with the rented commode. "Oh, empty. Molly got it when she brought your breakfast."

Garrett stared. He hadn't seen her do that. Wished she hadn't.

* * *

The next Sunday, with a light, spring dew sparkling on the grass and the air alive with the morning songs of robins, wrens, and the sharp calls of the ever-present blue jays, Garrett eased back and sank into cushions on the porch rocking chair. Will and Michael stepped back, smiling.

"Not so hard, Dad," Michael said to Will. "I think we've got this carrying thing down."

Garrett snorted. "I could have walked down. Going up is the problem."

"You're probably right, Pop. But doctor's orders. No stairs. Period." Will opened the screen door for Molly who balanced Heather in one arm and her Bible and the diaper bag in the other.

A few minutes later Michael and Molly left for church. Sarah, Will's wife, brought out cups of mint tea.

"Thank you," Garrett said. "Are you and Hettie coming out to sit?"

Sarah turned her face away and wiped her eyes. Turning back, she patted Garrett's shoulder. "I've a few more things to get ready for dinner, Pop."

Garrett rocked a while, then leaned back, closing his eyes. The freshness of the air filled his soul with hope. Hettie would get well, they'd plant the garden, and all the family would come for the summer reunion.

* * *

He startled a moment when Will shifted on the porch swing.

"Nothing like spring air for a nap, Pop. Church should be letting out soon." Will reached over and patted Garrett's knee. "Pot roast today, with rhubarb pie."

"Hettie cut the rhubarb yesterday, I reckon," Garrett said. "She told me it's been up for two weeks."

Will cleared his throat. "Pop, you're remembering last spring with Ma still alive."

"Stop, Will. Stop right now. I know what Hettie said. She made that pie this morning. I smelled it."

"Pop." Will sighed. "Calm down. We all miss her."

Garrett rocked forward in the chair. He stood, grabbed the porch railing, and lurched toward the stairs leading down to the yard.

"Pop, stop! You'll fall. What in the heck are you doing?"

"Hettie's out there now. She needs help." Garrett shook off Will's arm and took another step.

Michael pulled into the parking area across from the side yard. He jumped out of the car and raced toward his father and grandfather.

Sarah rushed from the kitchen and grabbed Garrett's arm. "Pop, come back. Dinner's almost ready."

Michael put his arms around Garrett. "Gramp, time to eat. Wait 'til Molly tells you what Heather did in church."

Garrett returned Michael's hug. "Glad you could come, Michael. Hettie will be pleased. She made a rhubarb pie, you know."

Will put his arm around his father. "Time to eat, Pop."

With Michael on one side and Will on the other, they guided Garrett into the dining room.

* * *

Monday. At least Garrett thought it was Monday. Other than Sunday when he was carried downstairs to sit in the parlor or out on the porch, all the days were the same. Molly opened the door and Michael carried in a tray.

"Hungry, Gramp?" Molly's cheerful voice followed Michael through the door.

Garrett grunted. Will and Michael, Molly, too, had all talked nonstop yesterday at dinner about church, the farm, the neighbors, everything but what Garrett wanted to talk about. Where was Hettie? Had they spirited her off to some hospital without telling him?

Michael held Garrett's elbow when he moved from the rocking chair to his desk. "Molly used Nana's recipe for the meatloaf, Gramp. Should be good."

He settled Garrett in the desk chair and sat on Garrett's bed, his own plate filled with the meatloaf, scalloped potatoes, and green beans.

"Never saw Hettie use a recipe for meatloaf or anything else." Garrett scooped a bite onto his fork. He chewed, smiled. "It's good, Molls. You got it right."

"Nana told me how she made it before she . . ." Molly's voice faded. "I asked her to. No one could cook like Nana."

Garrett lifted another bite of meatloaf, then set down his fork. "She's been singing that song about the cherry with no stone." He continued eating. "Hettie must be in the nursery. Do you see her, Molly? Does Hettie sit in that walnut rocker I made with the pink and white quilt over her lap?"

Molly looked at Michael. For a second, Michael frowned, then forked up some potatoes. Molly smiled. "No, Gramp. I haven't seen her. Haven't heard the song either."

From across the hall, they heard, "Mama, Mama."

Michael laughed. "Heather waited until you finished a meal. Imagine that!"

Molly called out. "Coming, sweetie." She stood and carried her empty plate toward the open door, then turned. "Abby's coming today. I'll ask her about that song. I'm sure she'll remember."

"Abby?"

"Yes, Spencer's girl. She's been away to school."

Garrett's fork hung in midair, and he stared again out the window. "Abby. Spencer's girl. Our girl after Margery died. She's coming, you say?"

The metal springs on Garrett's antique oak bed squeaked as Michael rose to leave. "Yes, around five she said when she called yesterday. I'll come up again before I go out. In case you want back in bed." He looked at the commode. "Or need anything else. The field's half done. Might finish today if the rain holds off."

After Michael left, Garrett pushed the potatoes and beans around on his plate. They tasted fine. He just couldn't seem to work up an appetite. No wonder. Sitting and sleeping all day. What must Hettie think?

* * *

Abby pulled into the long driveway leading up to Gramp's farm. Her cousin Michael had told her the ruts were passable. The spring rains had mostly come and gone. If she steered carefully and went slow, she wouldn't bottom out and ruin the oil pan on the old Rambler. Dad had given her the car when she started her senior year. She had explained about the student teaching assignment over in the next county. The school was pre-K through grade four in a building more like a house than a school. Fifteen first and second graders together in one room and sixteen third and fourth pupils in another. Grady's Run Primary was the smallest school in Preston County, and a bit of a drive from Morgantown, but

Abby had relished the rural placement. Reminded her of home. Now, she was finished with student teaching and could move back to the farm.

Michael met her on the front porch.

"Glad to see you, Abby. Gramp's been sleeping most of the day, but when he finds out you're here, I'm guessing he'll rouse up." Michael took Abby's backpack and bookbag.

Something in Michael's voice caused Abby to reach out and take his arm. "What's wrong? Is his heart worse?"

"Doc says he's about the same." He stared off toward the fields a moment, then said, "Sometimes he doesn't remember Nana is dead. Asks where she is."

"Oh . . ." The word faded in Abby's throat. She coughed and said, "He misses her so much."

"When Dad and I carried him downstairs yesterday, he and Dad sat on the porch while Molly and I went to church. Gramp got up suddenly and tried to go down the stairs. Said he wanted to go find Nana. Dad caught his arm before he fell, but Gramp was pretty angry. Accused Dad of keeping Nana away from him."

Abby released Michael's arm and pulled him into a hug. "I'm so sorry. I hope I can help."

"Once he sees you . . . well, I'm sure it will." On the landing leading to the second floor, Michael turned. "Your room's all fixed up and ready."

Abby thanked him and went through the dining room to the kitchen.

"Hi, Molly. How's Miss Heather this afternoon?" The baby looked up at Abby, her big brown eyes curious.

"Lookee here, Heather. Your cousin Abby, all the way from Morgantown."

The baby gurgled something and reached out her hand. "More," she said, pointing at the cut-up apple in the bowl Molly held just out of reach.

Molly put four more pieces on the highchair's tray. Heather's tiny fingers picked up an apple piece and put it in her mouth.

"You all still have apples?"

"Northern Spy. Only ones left. Two bushels. Michael says we'll be eating them until next harvest in October. 'Course, we'll have the summer apples come late July."

"What's that smell? Pie?"

Molly put a few more apple pieces on the baby's tray and gave Abby a hug. "Wanted something homemade for your visit, sweetie. I know how you loved Nana's apple pie."

Abby was halfway up the stairs when Molly, her voice softened, called after her. "Abby, Gramp says he sees Nana and hears her singing. Thought you should know."

Turning and retracing her steps, Abby paused a moment at Molly's serious face. "Michael told me. After Nana died, I thought I had seen her in the strangest places. The Kroger store, walking near my dorm in the snow."

Molly squeezed her hand. "Ah, honey. I don't know what to say."

Abby swallowed. "I saw a counselor. She helped me realize that when I thought I saw Nana, it was like a wish. From grief, yes, and love. If Gramp believes he sees and hears Nana, it may comfort him."

"Wish that were true. But he's showing a lot of anger. Shouts. Bangs his cane on the floor."

Abby pulled Molly close. "How about you? Holding up to all the extra work?"

Tears flowed down Molly's cheeks. "I'm trying. We were okay until that heart episode and Gramp decided to stay upstairs. I thought the bed in the parlor was a perfect solution. There was room for Heather's playpen. The two of them on this floor would have saved all that up and down carrying."

"Dad's helping me move next Saturday. I'll be here full time then. I know you all eat with Gramp upstairs. I'll take over, Molly, I promise."

Molly sniffled. "Go on. Heather's banging on her tray."

When Abby reached the second-floor hall, she peeked in her own room first. Michael had put her bookbag on the desk, her backpack on the floor near the closet. The dark wood of her Jenny Lind spool bed contrasted with her white bedspread.

The window was open, and the spring breeze brought in the smell of lilacs. The white dotted Swiss curtains fluttered. Abby breathed in the scent of the lilacs, remembering how last May she and Nana had cut so many of the heavy blossoms that Nana had put them in a large pickle crock for a vase. Some fresh flowers for Gramp's room would bring spring inside. Slipping off her shoes, she found some slippers on a closet shelf and tiptoed down the hall.

* * *

In Gramp's room Abby sat in the rocker, its soft squeak and swoosh, rhythmic, comforting. One of Nana's songs slipped into her head, and she hummed along. "The Riddle Song." Remembering Nana's clear high voice, Abby sang, *"I gave my love a cherry that had no stone. I gave my love a chicken that had no bone. I gave my love a story that had no end. I gave my love a baby with no crying."*

An old, old song, Nana had said. A country song. A mountain song.

* * *

Garrett awoke and stared at the young woman in the hickory rocker he had made when Hettie and he had their first born. A part of his mind knew he was looking at his granddaughter, Abby, but for a few precious moments, he had seen Hettie when he'd first brought her home. The same auburn hair and high cheekbones, the same sprinkle of freckles across the bridge of her nose. She gazed out the window just as he did every day now. She stopped singing and looked at him through Hettie's gray-green eyes.

"Hettie." Garrett's voice was a whisper, blanketed in loss.

"Hi, Gramp." Abby rose from the chair, kissed his cheek, and sat on Garrett's bed. "School's out. I did well. I've already interviewed to teach back here. I want to live with you again."

"Abby . . . Abby," Garrett said, his voice stronger. "Of course." He paused. "Hettie will be pleased. Did you see her? I smelled apple pie. Figured she was baking."

Abby took his hand in both of hers. "Molly made a pie. Just like Nana before she died. It does smell great."

"Died? Hettie is here. She sings." Garrett's voice rose. "Why do you all say that? She's been sick, that's all. Hettie would never leave me without saying goodbye."

He turned his face into his pillow. After a moment he turned back. "Abby? You're here, dear. Where's Spencer and Margery? Nothing pleases us like having all of you home."

Abby leaned over Garrett and kissed him once again. "Would you like to get up, Gramp? Sit in the rocker? I can help you."

"In a minute, yes. But I can get up by myself. I need to get back in shape, help with the farm. Not fair to put it all on Michael."

* * *

Ten years earlier on another morning in May, Hettie slipped into Garrett's room. Her steps quiet, she lit the oil lamp on the oak desk. They had electric in all the rooms now, but Garrett had insisted on keeping his father's oil lamp. Hettie had never seen him turn on the ceiling light or the floor lamp in the corner. She looked at the bed. Empty. She laughed as a sudden flush warmed her face. Her thoughts of a quick hug, warm kiss, and maybe more evaporated. When had Garrett moved out of their marriage bed to his father's old room? Babies. That answered the when and the why.

Garrett had risen before the dawn all the time she'd known him. "Sometimes you get the baby to sleep beside you, and I need to get up to see to the milking. I won't disturb your sleep, my love."

Of course, they'd gotten together, quite often in fact. Six children proved that. Humming "*I gave my love a cherry*," Hettie made the bed and opened the curtains. The sunrise peaked over the eastern ridge. She heard the tractor and saw Garrett going through the gate to the upper field. Last night he'd told her he planned to make one more pass with the harrow and then start the planting. Corn. All twelve acres.

It was nearly eight o'clock when Garrett came in for breakfast. Hettie loaded up his plate with flapjacks and ham, poured his coffee. Before he sat, Garrett enfolded her in his arms.

"Been thinking about you, my treasure. With Junie Mae teaching up in Ohio and the other'uns all married and spread out, 'bout time we got back in the same bed."

"Hmmm," Hettie whispered as she nuzzled his neck. "Might be I been thinking the same thing."

* * *

Two months later with the corn already a foot high, Hettie heard the crunch of tires on the gravel Garrett had spread in that low spot in front of the barn. From the porch she saw Spencer's blue Ford. Her son walked around to the passenger side and opened the door. Instead of his wife Margery, their daughter Abby slid slowly off the seat and took her father's hand.

"Dear Lord," Hettie choked. "She must be sick."

Hettie had reached the bottom step when Abby broke into a run and grabbed Hettie around the waist. Sobs racked her body, gangly and thin just like her father had been at age eleven.

Spencer put his arms around both his mother and daughter. "I know you just got a phone line, but I couldn't call with this news. Margery's gone, an accident on Route 50, two nights ago. She died this morning. I'll get Pop to come in and tell you both. Don't think I can tell it twice."

* * *

Margery's funeral came and went. Neighbors and family from all over the mountain and surrounding counties turned out. The wake was in Garrett and Hettie's parlor, the service in the little church in the valley. For the rest of the summer, Abby stayed with Hettie and Garrett, Spencer's old room refreshed with a white, dotted Swiss coverlet and matching curtains.

On one of Spencer's visits, he sat with Hettie on the front porch, fresh coffee in both their cups.

"I can keep the house in Elkins, Ma, get a housekeeper and cook. If I didn't need to travel so much, I could do all that myself. I did, you know. Help out. It wasn't all on Margery. She had a job too." His voice broke. Hettie rose from her rocker and sat beside him on the porch swing. She held him close, murmuring his name.

"A housekeeper won't do, Spencer," she finally said. "Our Abby needs to be with family. Hard enough to lose her mother, don't disconnect her from us."

Spencer put both hands on his mother's shoulders. "Abby will never be disconnected from you and Pop." Once again, his throat closed, and he choked. "But . . ."

Hettie put a finger up to his lips. "You forget about that. The cancer's gone." She laughed. "I'm as healthy as a horse."

Abby rushed up the porch steps. "Look, Nana. Daddy. I found him behind the barn. Those nasty crows were pecking at the nest. This little guy was the only one left." She looked down and swallowed back a sob. "The rest were all dead. He was off in the grass, trying to get away."

The tiny rabbit had nestled into Abby's shirt, where she'd folded it up to make a pocket. Spencer brushed a lock of Abby's hair back from her face.

"I'll find a box. We'll need an eyedropper. If I remember right, goat's milk is best. I'll drive down to Bailey's farm. Richard keeps goats." His face serious, he said, "Don't get your hopes up. Orphaned wild rabbits don't usually survive, even with care."

But survive, he did. The wild rabbit that Abby named Blossom grew, feasted on the kitchen trimmings placed in his bowl or on Abby's outstretched hand. The summer ended and Abby enrolled in the school in the valley.

* * *

Garrett wasn't sure what awakened him. Mingling with the smell of the lilacs his granddaughter had placed on his desk was a softer scent of roses. Hettie. His dream had been of the two of them sometime in the summer after their spring wedding. The power of their coupling had taken over the routine of their lives. They'd managed to break away from their bedroom to see to the chores or visit with family or neighbors who popped in to sit a spell. The joy of being together had fueled a fire in Garrett he had never known existed. Hettie too. And that bond had lasted through the years. Enriched with children, the spark between them had not diminished.

The darkness of the night was complete, unbreakable. If the stars were out, Garrett couldn't see them. The curtains were closed, the evening night sounds long stilled. He swung his legs off the bed and found his cane. Now that he was looking toward the hall, he could see a faint line of light under his door from one of the night lights Molly had put at the top of the stairs. Cautious, wanting to hold on to his memories, Garrett stepped toward Hettie's room. He passed Molly and Michael's room across from the nursery.

The next room had been Spencer's, now Abby's. Her door was closed, but he could hear soft breathing, a few murmured words. He came to the wide, oak door of Hettie's room, their room. Within, Hettie's mother's quilt covered the large four-poster bed. A double wedding ring quilt, Hettie had told him. The different shades of blue and tiny prints of yellow and green all blended into gray in the darkened room.

As he stood there, the moon slipped from behind a cloud. Light poured into the room from the casement window, bright enough that Garrett could see more of the colors in the quilt and the shapes of the Highboy dresser and Hettie's grandmother's dressing table. He sat on the bed, fingered the lace-trimmed pillow.

"Hettie, my sweet, my precious love. Where have you gone?"

Garrett lay down on the quilt and buried his face in the pillow. He shut away the memory of Hettie's sickness, the cancer that had riddled her body until she wasted to skin and bones. The family had gathered, all four sons and two daughters, every single grandchild, some staying here in the house, some with neighbors, aunts, uncles, friends.

* * *

On her last night, a week after Christmas, he lay beside her, the heirloom quilt covering them both. Hettie's hand fingered a thin strand of her hair. A single tear flowed from the corner of her eye and down her cheek.

Garrett cradled her face in his hands. "I see your hair the way it was, dear heart. Long and wavy, silver the last few years. Sometimes I see your auburn locks grown way past your shoulders. You are and always will be beautiful."

Hettie had squeezed his hand, and a small chuckle escaped. "You always knew how to sweet talk me."

"You gave me, all of us, joy. Life. Beauty." Garrett's voice trembled, and he pulled her close. "There's no happiness without you, my dearest love. If you cannot stay, then I will come too. Soon."

The memories of Hettie's last moments were vivid, both gentle and strong. On the quilt that smelled of Hettie's rosewater, Garrett closed his eyes and listened. Hettie's sweet singing voice was muted, distant. Instead of "The Riddle Song" she sang a hymn that had been her mother's favorite. At Garrett's request, the choir at the church funeral had sung the first three verses, many in attendance joining in. Garrett hummed a moment then whispered, "Hettie, the darkness deepens. I miss you so."

He prayed, "Dear Lord, abide with me. Help me find my Hettie."

A dull pain blossomed and grew in Garrett's chest as a cool breeze moved through the room. Garrett felt Hettie's hand stroke his arm, then his face. Her voice whispered his name, loving him, welcoming him home.

A Sunday Morning

That trap—
Shouldn't have
Checked it before heading
Off to church, but we did.
No groundhog—worse,

A skunk, hind leg clasped
Firmly, stared with beady eyes
As we approached garden's edge

Standing there in our wool
Suits knowing it inhumane
To wait, Uncle Ralph said,
Sam, get the gun.

Meaning, of course,
An old Remington 22
By the fireplace—
The double barrel
Was fetched instead.

Uncle Ralph glanced at his watch,
Shrugged his shoulders,
Reluctantly accepted the shotgun,
Turned, aimed and fired,
We'll take care of it when we get back.

For one eternal hour
Seated in the pews

Of that small church
An uncomfortable congregation
Imagined the sulfurous
Stench of hell was upon them. . . .

We feigned innocence,
Knowing it was really upon us.

Mickey Mouse Voices a Preference for John Ford Westerns Starring John Wayne

I have likes and dislikes, thanks to Walt Disney. I like
The Searchers, Wayne framed in entryway skyscape.

Wayne is soaringly oversized. He cocks a Henry rifle
in a swinging-motion-click of Manifest Destiny and

Red Scare anti-Communism. Whatever retribution
he interrupts, John Wayne / Ethan Edwards, it's

nothing compared to what the settlers have done,
believing God to be on their side while exercising

dominion premised on the killing of children.
Minnie always asks me what your problem is,

White America, why Difference is such a target.
I say, You ever see the way John Wayne sashays?

You can't walk like that and be an American man
who fucks heterosexual women who worship Jesus.

You have to be a movie star in a John Ford western
on every screen in nineteen fifty-six to pull that off.

Stronger

Mein junger Sohn fragt mich: Soll ich Geschichte lernen?
—Bertold Brecht

My younger daughter asked me
      while writing a paper on antisemitism:
"The teacher told us to come up
      with arguments against our own theses.
Papa, I'm confused,
      what should I tell him?"

"You tell him," I said, "there is
      no argument against truth.
Tell him, a thesis in favor of prejudice
      would be an impossible ruse."

Six months later my younger daughter
      asked me, after getting her history syllabus:
"There are many kinds of prejudice here,
      but not a word about Jew-hatred.
I feel like we've been thrown under the bus.
      Papa, what should I say to the teacher?"

Say to her that selective justice
      is a form of bigotry.
You say to her, they cannot hide the evidence—
      no matter how hard they try.

On the eve of her Bat Mitzvah
      I asked my younger daughter:

"Taniusha, how do you feel?"

She put her hand on my shoulder—
lightly, gently like my older angel.

"I'm good, Papa," she answered. "I'm stronger."

Multilingual

An app on my phone
promises to teach me 39 languages—
the work of a lifetime
to learn them all.

Out my window, a chickadee sings its name—
chick-a-dee-dee-dee!
How cute, I used to think,
until I learned its name is a warning,
an alarm call heeded by many a creature
to flee or freeze.

Feathered and furry souls alike
know this lingua franca,
but I do not, and I think
how many languages we humans
have still to learn.

It's Not There

The new comet, like the last &, likely, next:
an absence. Hills surround the city
like judges in their shadow robes,
heads a haze jaundiced by under-glow.
They've sentenced me to lack
of the miraculous. This one's green,

I've read. It goes unseen.
I walk my lump of earth & grass,
never spot the cartoon villain's eyelash,
the punk rocker's hairdo,
the poorly-written semicolon
drawn in Crayon. If it exists,

it's like a god: invisible, unwelcoming.
I name this comet *Nothingness*.
I name it *Hope Betrayed Again*.
The news advises, *Look near the horizon*.
Might as well say, *Stretch your arms &*
swim through the sky to Mars.

Book Review

Pennsylvania Furnace

Julie Swarstad Johnson (Greensboro: Unicorn Press, 2019)
$18.00, softcover, Smyth-sewn binding. $25.00, hardcover.
ISBN 978-0-87775-058-1, 91 pp.

How do we love the land, even as we participate in doing damage to it? How do we honor those who have come before us, even as we acknowledge the destructive hungers they advanced?

These are the questions that came to me as I read *Pennsylvania Furnace*, the first book of poems by Julie Swarstad Johnson. In poems that weave effortlessly, sometimes magically, between past and present, Johnson considers the significance of resource extraction in American lives. Her poems step back and forth across the continent, juxtaposing the Arizona desert-cities of the speaker's home with the ridges and valleys of central Pennsylvania, where her parents are from. And while her connection to those ridges and valleys is familial, it's also accidental, and personal: it's there that she finds the remnants of Pennsylvania's booming 19th-century ironmaking industry. Captivated by that industry's echoes, she goes on a journey to learn about those old furnace stacks that stand "like lone towers left from fortresses / by the roadside." Like students of this regional history who came before her, Johnson suggests that although she's from elsewhere, ". . . perhaps my foreign eyes can see / what you have grown accustomed to, what you / have overlooked" (26).

And it's true. I grew up and still live in northern Appalachia but seeing it through Johnson's "foreign eyes" is a revelation. In carefully researched persona poems, she speaks in the voices of people who lived and worked in Pennsylvania's iron villages, who kept places like Centre

Furnace, Greenwood Furnace, and others blazing through the night. She meditates on not only the difficulty but the beauty of these lives. One poem describes the "hellish light" of a relentlessly productive furnace, the "red flush at midnight / that seeps in at the edges of dreams" (7), while another imagines "the scorch of metal pooling silver-bright" (31). Her newcomer's eye also vivifies the ecologies of northern Appalachia: She speaks to barn swallows, describes a cicada's "body unfurling out slick / with wings pale as a glass / just filled with wine" (50), and imagines a river walking up into the sky, where "It remembers the riverbed / crush of sand and pebbles rolling along / against its electric skin." More often than not, Johnson's attention to the beauty of history and to that of ecology are twined, as in the poem "Passage," where "The sky,

> a river, has reached the charcoal flat,
> perfect, rounded scar in the woods,
> and just another ridge away, the old growth.
> A hornet's nest has brought it
> to this encircled openness, the vaulted space,
> shaped by the rain scissoring the canopy. (42)

Yet beauty, in these poems, is a fraught subject. When the poet imagines a mule team pulling ore, their "ears cupped / to hold in the bell's songs", she quickly amends the image, writing, "Pity yourself, // you who hear them as songs" (19). Again and again this speaker questions her own perceptions of beauty, her temptation to romanticize lives and industries inextricable from environmental degradation. Johnson is willing to admit that she sometimes finds damage beautiful: "who could see the coal coming forth and not / feel moved" (52) asks one persona poem— and, even more remarkable, she's equally willing to name that she feels shame for finding it so. She wrestles to look past "that easily damaged gilt / of what I want to see" (39) and acknowledges her complicity in what she laments: "smog I inherited, smog / I rage against from / my own car while // the newscasters chant / *heat inversion, / no burn day*" (28-29). I was particularly moved by the poem "A Brief History of Illumination by Gas Lamp," which weaves a complicated thread between the gas-lit night shift in Manchester, England's early-19th-century textile factories; contemporary extraction fields in North Dakota alight in the dark, burning off superfluous natural gas; and the poet herself, hanging blankets in the windows at night to keep out the streetlight.

It's hard not to think of climate change while reading this book, even though so many of its poems take place over a hundred years ago, in a moment we may be tempted to think of as far from the devastating realities of today. Yet it was clearly the hungers of past centuries that led to this moment, and *Pennsylvania Furnace*, for all its "gutterman's clogs" and charcoal flats, feels achingly timely.

I mentioned shame some lines ago; it strikes me now that, in the context of our human relationship to the earth, shame is a good thing to be honest about and to name. It's not an emotion that comes up often in conversations about climate change, although it should. I wonder if that's because science—the field to which much mainstream rhetoric has entrusted all truth about global warming—isn't very good at tending to people's emotional lives. We need poetry for that, and perhaps we even need a frankly religious poet. In this book, we have a speaker who praises and doubts like a pilgrim, and indeed her thinking is taut with pilgrimage and exodus, with rich and surprising Biblical allusions. "Like God / at the beginning," Johnson writes,

>   the pecan trees
> divide water from water, a new expanse
> of heaven dotted with sweetness
> in their arms. Yes—I am worried
> over the coming world. Somewhere, someone
> consults figures of groundwater, river water,
> average rainfall to approve
> a new water line to the groves. Yes—
> I anticipate the warm, sweet nut
> weighing on my tongue. (59)

Hers is a voice alive with all the complexities and contradictions one wants from a spiritual thinker.

Like such a thinker, the poems in *Pennsylvania Furnace* are provocative, and subtle. Yet the question that smolders at the heart of the book isn't subtle; these poems seem to ask, finally, where it is that we live—in a world of paradise or destruction, heaven or hell? And if there is an answer, Johnson puts it this way: "The mountains might never look / so beautiful as they do tonight, // on fire" (72).

Additional note:

Johnson's attention to northern Appalachia extends beyond this first book. In 2018 she served as Artist in Residence at Gettysburg National Military Park, an experience that fueled her chapbook *Orchard Light*, which documents the lives of pacifist Pennsylvanians during the Civil War. Published in 2019 by Seven Kitchens Press, *Orchard Light* extends the range of Johnson's spiritual complexity, posing questions about violence, peace, and nationhood that are as unexpectedly timely as the poems in *Pennsylvania Furnace*.

Myth

A myth is a story
that lights a dark corner,

and there are many
dark corners here—
dark rock, dark waters,
dark shadows
in a dark wood.

The myth begins
when creatures enter.

I went into the wood.
A butterfly met me
and ushered me out
at the end.

In between, rain
drip-dripped
through the leaves,
the earth tipped
but did not spill me,

a family of deer flashed
along the edge
of the wood, flashed
along the edge
of sight.

A dark bird called
and wove through the trees.

I call this myth.

Just beyond the road,
look: the woods begin,
the wild fields
and creeks
with their wild
rock sentinels.

Myth grows there.

Take your longings
and go.
You will hear it
singing.

Don't look back.

A Holy Greening Power

It was the green of wild things—
the cloud this morning. It sang
of lizards' skins and the insides
of turtle shells, of snake venom
and the light right before a tornado

spins into a mythic beast. It spoke
to me of its longing to become
rain, of its urge for a thundering,
to let loose a great heaving sob
of all it had seen before it got here.

As it passed, it dreamed cloud dreams
over me, hummed the same tone
as the ringing in my ears, quieted
when just overhead and then,
just as the sun snuck beneath

the cloud's green glower, let loose
a shower of glistering prisms.
Then it moved on, leaving blue
and a sweet smell of what rotting brings
to spring, of fresh gunpowder,

of the music that calls the skunks
and bunnies out in great numbers,
and me to the garden to fence
the peas, to rake the chickweed
into windrows to prepare for

the planting of greens, which will grow
in human-tamed hues, will preen
with a vanity only known to cultivated
things, which, like me are too tender
to survive the storm that is coming.

Wendy McVicker

Toward a New Conference of All Beings

Turtle-beings swim to meet me.
We gaze at each other
through bleared glass.

If they are exiled
from their home, then so
am I, and we each need
to find our way back

through wind and weather,
through wildness
and wilderness confined
to the place that spawned us

where once again we will speak
—as we did long ago—
and call out our names
in our own tongue,

braiding our voices
like the river's currents
into one mighty flow.

All the Information I Have about Myself Is from Forged Documents

—Vladimir Nabokov, *Despair*

My father changed a date on his birth certificate to enlist in
the Army—or so he said, over and over, like it was his reality
and he wanted it shared. It might have been, too, if his mother
hadn't confronted him, straightening herself in the red rolled-
leather of the backseat of a Cadillac, saying: *I'm pretty sure*

I know when you were born. And addressing him, my father,
in a way it was easy to grasp why the consensus of opinion
was she needed institutionalized. The heart of the story is,
she got sent off to a sanitarium after my father was born
for confronting the man who'd helped get her pregnant.

I knew my grandmother pursued Bob Beach with a .45—
she had emptied the clip and was reloading, cussing him,
Bob, with every dissenting breath. A pissed-off woman.
There was mention of a phone pole. Hurried climbing.
Mother's oldest sister, my aunt Blanche, told the stories

of our family over meals in her row house in Kentucky.
Blanche liked my father. She said that I should trust him.
She said his mother (and she searched for the right word)
had a habit of misremembering. Blanche described shock
treatments. Said my great grandmother had locked her

adult daughter, Susan, in an upstairs room after news
of the pregnancy. Blanche could tell a story. Theatrically
crowned in silvery Pall Mall cigarette smoke, she said

my grandmother wasn't about to send the source of her
humiliation to some Perdition where spiritual reckoning

is the stock in trade, never you mind pity and forgiveness.
My aunt had seen my grandmother shoot. Shotguns, pistols.
In particular, a slag heap practice session left her impressed.
Pop bottle after pop bottle, Mason jar after Mason jar—she
said that if Susan had wanted Bob dead, he would be dead.

Fit for Duty

Microwave telescope dishes ready for action at
the National Radio Observatory in Green Bank, WV

They line the slopes of grass-green
banks like a row of soldiers, a squad
arrayed in solemn stance, all fourteen
orphaned from platoon of metal.

Their triple legs fold as telescope tubes
slipping inside each other, working
as one. Strapped with backpacks of
batteries; power meters locked, loaded

to the LNB, the dish head bows smartly,
mottled gray and black for covert ops
in a different kind of jungle warfare.
Headsets hidden, but for the mouthpiece,

like a horn positioned to the offset march
of radio waves—ready for black heat, and static
noise of sky.

The Wayfinder

Every map starts somewhere . . .

I crouch to the ground, the blades of grass tickling my chin as I press flat. The warm sun, high and bright in a perfect, cloudless blue sky, beats down on my shoulders as I stare through the thick foliage. I can smell the grass and the soil, the scent rising to my nostrils, driven upward by the summertime heat.

My eyes work to penetrate the gloom in front of me—deep, pooled shadows at the base of the brush. I clench my teeth.

I can't see him.

"Hold on, hold on," my guide whispers. He stares at the same spot—he's blessed with a lot more experience in these matters than I, and like any other novice, I can't help but feel ultimately confused about what he's seeing and what I'm not. His voice is low, urgent. He wants me to succeed, but he's been down this road a few times before and he knows when to execute and when to stay patient.

It's much harder for me . . . but I'm a fast study, and so I break concentration on the spot and focus instead on my guide. He crouches, still as a statue, staring at that same spot, gray-blue eyes focused and sharp, slicing through the gloom. His eyes crinkle at the corners, blending in with a network of weathering and wrinkles that he's accumulated through his years of toil and grit.

I hear the insects buzzing, along with more distant birdsong. My heart pounds in my chest, in my ears, almost so loud that it drowns other sounds around me, and I'm sure that my quarry can hear my own heart, betraying my position. I feel the reflected heat from the ground through my shirt. The blades of grass are cool against the rest of these sensations, the sun warm on my neck, grit in the skin of my palms and knees.

"There he is! Get him!" the guide exclaims.

The animal bursts from the pooled shadow, dashing for freedom by splitting the space between us. It's the worst situation imaginable for a close-in stalk, with a creature charging hell-bent for leather and inveigling the hunters into a crossfire. This is where a seasoned guide *really* earns his pay, particularly when charged with overseeing the inexperienced novice.

"Get him!" the guide says again, excitement in his voice.

And that's when I see him. I rear back, cupping my hands to catch the spring peeper frog bounding between us.

I miss.

I scramble, too excited to be upset at missing my chance. "Where is he? Where is he?" That's when the little frog springs again, making for the bright surface of the concrete driveway.

The guide gets to his feet, loping after the tiny, jumping, evasive pipsqueak. We get there at the same time and he cups my hands with his own. I can feel the little amphibian charge the confines of its fleshy cage a couple of times, then he halts.

"Okay, okay . . . careful now," my guide says. "He'll want you to think he isn't there and let up, and he'll get away."

"Okay," I say, my heart pounding wildly in my four-year old chest.

My grandfather struggles to his feet again and dutifully retrieves the small glass jar, already furnished with a twig and a few blades of grass, the commonly known accouterments for such an amphibian guest. The lid's already been equipped with a half-dozen or so air holes, and Grandpa, kneeling again, twists the lid.

"Now, keep your hands around the outside of the jar and I'll set this down on top of him."

I do just that and the frog, sitting now as he undoubtedly was just thirty seconds before, puffs his cheeks out in a harrumph. We tilt the jar and the little guy tumbles to the bottom, rights himself in an instant, and then stares, irritated, out at the two human faces—one old, one impossibly young—looking back at him through the rippled glass. He's not much bigger than half a cigarette lighter. Even in my small hands, he looked tiny.

My guide twists the top back on the jar and grins at me. "Good job!" he says. He ambles to a raised split in the driveway, and he carefully puts the jar down. He sits next to it, and then pats a handkerchief on his forehead and upper lip, dabbing at the perspiration. He looks down at the frog, still sitting morosely in the jar, and chuckles. Then, still smiling, he looks up at me and winks. My first hunting trip, midday in my grand-parents' front yard in Johnstown under a painfully bright blue summer sky, would set the hook for decades to come.

This is one of the few clear, real memories I have of my grandfa-ther, but I must think that this early experience shaped me nearly as much as anything in my life. Of course, as things would unfold, my own father would play a huge—and an absolutely much larger—role in my affinity for hunting and fishing. This first experience with my maternal grandfather—a man who, to my knowledge, never "hunted" in the way we would understand it—likely created in me an easier path towards a taste for the pursuit.

I think about my grandfather every day still, more than forty years after his death from a massive heart attack at the far too-young age of 66. I know that, at some level, I'm taller now than he ever was, but that just doesn't seem real to me. To me, he was a towering figure, a retired steelworker and general foreman . . . also the guy who stalked my first wild animal with me under that warm summer sun.

Not only do I think of my grandfather decades later, but I also know that I'd give nearly anything to see him for one more day. I would expect many of us might feel the same way—give anything to have one more day with a person we lost too soon. The conversation, for me, would span decades. He would be amazed, delighted, proud. Of course, this thought of mine—usually arising unbidden amidst an otherwise fine day—ruins my outlook on things for quite a while. The impossibility of it, coupled with the immense *frustration* of the impossibility, gives the sense of loss a weight and power, an unstoppable force. The other problem: everything fades. The memories of my grandfather are not as strong as I'd like them to be, and I suspect that they fade more with each passing year, the color draining from the memory, the lines fading, the vision dimming, the sounds growing softer and more distant.

Perhaps it's the northern Appalachia highlands that have guided me as well; some places in the world have taller mountains and deeper valleys, but the complex wrinkles that are these hills and valleys command—or allow—one to get lost, whether one wants to or not. I've had opportunities to move away, far away, permanently away, but I've never taken them—not to London, Hong Kong, or Johannesburg. The map of my fate, or at least of the twists and turns in my life, has led on strange and twisted paths, leading off the page, doubling back, confused, turning, questioning, wondering, but never, ever answering.

All the travel gave me knowledge that there is something to seeing a new place for the first time—a possibility and promise of comfort and acquired familiarity. If a positive experience, it etches a personal map onto the heart and mind. For that matter, so does a negative experience—in that personal map of heart and mind, etched are the big bold letters of "Here There Be Tigers." Either way, there's learning and enrichment, awareness, and appreciation. The map gains contours and curves, roads which may or may not lead anywhere.

Throughout the travels, all that I ever really wanted to do was to get back to my own hills and valleys. The green forests blanket the hills against an impossibly iridescent blue sky in the summer; the radiant explosion of astonishing colors in September and October; the bleak leaden clouds of November frame those same trees, barren and bark red with soaking, cold rains; in winter—the heavy white snow falling, piling on the ground and tree boughs, frigid air so still and silent one can scarcely believe it. These are the skies and the scenes of memory and of dreams alike. It's taken my travel, however, to make me see my home for what it is: my own spot on this strange and difficult map.

A different season, a different view: frozen and bare wintertime trees, shining white snow glowing on the hillsides. This is a new image, despite the familiarity implied. At the first traces of sunlight dawning from the southeast, the snow has a purple hue. I watch this, sipping coffee, looking over the woods and the ridges around my home in Bedford County. It's the day after a duck hunt on the upper Potomac with a couple of good friends, one a cop in western Maryland, the other a professor at Georgetown (who also hails from western Pennsylvania.)

The hunt had ended early, and we packed in the decoys and other gear, wading in the frigid water, the January smell of cold water and soaked rocks, along with the dry and almost smoky scent of the brush on the tiny islands in the middle of the channel. Small ice floes twirled and eased downstream around us, the water's coldness seeping through even the heavy waders. We took the Potomac upstream past Hancock, where we had put in, just to have a look at the new day. While cold, it wasn't as frigid as it could have been, and the day was bright and sunny, with that same stupefyingly pure blue sky, daring one to imagine that just several dozens of miles downriver, there's the crushing population of the Baltimore-DC megalopolis, my professional center, my other starting point for the map. Here on the river, however, there is none of that—just the water, the mountains, the woods.

A few small groups of geese and ducks took off and sped skyward as they heard us coming and watched us approach from around a bend, the dark-water river gently curving back and forth, the channel wide, with only a little ice and gentle downstream current. We exchanged hand waves with a pair of muskellunge fishermen lobbing dinner-plate size spoon lures into the river as we proceeded upstream. On both sides, Maryland and West Virginia, the hills rose steeper, both crowding in and elevating us, both the mark of a pathway and a gate. All the while, I was aware of my own house just on the other side of the ridge, just up there to the right, my own small and prized part of this knotted and difficult landscape. The sky burned bluer and bluer, delicate clouds high, wispy, and white, and just for a moment I had the impression of the river lifting us through the mountains and into the sky. These lands are both my home and the gateway to the world in which I make the map of my life. Decades ago, I thought the map was going to be neat and clear, the mark of a vision that well understands the world and captures it. I can see my grandfather smiling again, in that knowing way that I understand now so well.

Geography is a funny thing, but the contours are what must matter to a land-bound creature like me. I know these hills here, in Maryland, in West Virginia, in Pennsylvania, all a part of the first frontier, the Allegheny Front, Appalachia. I can recognize the ridges and hollows as readily as I can anything else in the world because it is here that I know *home*. I know that these mountains have been here for hundreds of millions of years, once towering like the Himalayas in the ancient, combined continent of Pangea. The rocks beneath my feet, under my home, are a billion years old, deep into the deepest times that defy comprehension. I know that the same ridges and hills are not just in Alabama, Pennsylvania, and Maine, but also the ancient hills and ridges in Scotland and Scandinavia. And yet they too have changed over a length of time incomprehensible to the human mind.

I have several framed century-or-more-old topographic maps of the area around my home, showing a handful of Pennsylvania counties: Somerset, Bedford, Fulton, Cambria, and their linkage to western Maryland. The old maps show the old trails before there were roads; they show the paths of trains on railway cuts now long gone and returned to the forest. So on that next morning at home, I pass by those framed maps and I think about the duck hunt and the jaunt upriver as I look out over the trees and sip my coffee, staring out at this still-endless forest, and I think about the could haves, the should haves, the what ifs, the map of my life, now ragged in edges and looking a bit too worn and thin in places. I see the sun rise in the east, each day roving from north to south and back over the course of a year, a cycle of billions of years. With each cycle, I see my grandfather and myself. Many evenings I can hear a coyote—sometimes several in a ghostly, yip-yip-yipping chorus—along with the great horned owls, showing the eternity of nature defying an extirpation driven by Europeans three hundred years earlier. The cycle of hunter and hunted is eternal; those of us who hunt will bow before the bond between the predator and the prey. Change always haunts all things, even these mountains.

But still, with the change, I build that personal map and find some new routes and intriguing paths that I hadn't tried before. The map may have more creases and wrinkles, but still it grows, with more notes and arrows pointing in different directions. At the same time, while I've roamed nearly everywhere, I cannot find any other home but this one; the gate still stands, connecting and separating alike.

At one time, very long ago, I thought I'd had a map of great clarity and pointing to solutions to all mysteries. No longer is this the case—it has become confused, often circular, with paths eating their own tails and leaving enormous swaths of territory blank and filled with the frightening unknown. I still don't have those answers despite the strange and sprawling map I've created. But I do have my hills, my streams, my woods, and my memories.

I do have the blessed security of that frog hunt with my grandfather, countless sunrises over the hills and sunsets behind them. My desired life path, an academic one, never materialized for me, but any of these other memories and experiences, time with my family and friends, are things that never would have been afforded to me had I used a different map. The different map would have, with virtual certainty, meant that I would have steered away from these hills and woods. I would not have had the morning of duck hunting, and I would not have had the time I've been able to spend with those most important to me.

Would my life have been better or worse? I have no way to know; this has been one of the more difficult elements for me to come to terms with—not only the not knowing, but the "what if" that would have been "better." At least, in my imagination and my projected memories from my 14-year-old self . . . a person who, in all reality, is as gone as my grandfather. Perhaps enough left to be a ghost, but no longer of this world.

Sometimes I will sit in the mausoleum housing the remains of my grandparents; I'll look at the beautiful white marble, the bronze plaques bearing name, birthdate, and death date. I think about what occurred in my grandfather's all too short 66 years, and how he may never have been able to imagine what that span of time would mean on me and my own map. The same mountains guard the mausoleum as much as they guard me.

I have the good fortune of living within a couple minutes' walk of the Eastern Continental Divide. I can literally stand with one foot on one side and know that the water on one side will run to the Chesapeake via the Juniata and Susquehanna, and the other to the Gulf of Mexico via some unnamed tributary creek hailing from Somerset County and running into Dark Shade—just now coming back to life decades after the end of heavy coal-mining and acid drainage—into the Stonycreek, thence into the Conemaugh, Kiskiminetas, Allegheny, Ohio, to the mighty Mississippi.

I'm blessed to be here, in this spot, the soles of my feet more secure and comfortable on these steep ridges and in the old hardwoods. I suppose that most of us must feel strange about where our lives have taken us from time to time . . . the unexpected, the unplanned, the unwelcome. Some find new ways. Some, I suppose, never find their way back from the strange turns, no matter how desperate they might be to come home . . . they become lost.

I've looked out from the sweeping ridge; the barren wintertime woods offer far greater visibility through the trees even as they offer less protection from a biting winter chill, a wind that seems to be constant here on the ridge even if the direction itself changes. These hills teem with trilling and chirping life during the peak of summer, but the cold of the winter winds can jerk tears from one's eyes and suck heat from one's core, no matter how well-dressed for the conditions. The hundreds of millions of years of life on these mountains have meant that they've seen the collapses of tropical rainforests blanketing the earth through ice ages until the industrial re-shaping one sees today. This has always been the way here; patrolling contested grounds, once from time immemorial until now, strip malls and housing developments in one vision and the real world—a forests, ridges, sky—in another. Still—a place to which I return, which beckons, despite however far I might roam.

The wayfinder might pay homage to those who have gone on without us, perhaps to other lands we have yet to see. This is a powerful revelation, at once a jagged, sharp reality carrying a powerful, subtle clarity: one isn't doing this alone. The hands of one's ancestors are on one's own map. The wayfinder must find new paths too, as a matter of course. The routes taken before may only be suggestions now. What my grandfather left for me, more than forty years ago now, is fuzzy, more about strong colors and feeling than well-defined lines of understanding. It instead became an emotional and spiritual truth about who and what I am.

My map, centered on these hills and rivers, sees it not as a has-been or backward territory; instead, the map's center has this spot as a bridge not only to go find new lands but also to find one's way home. I see now that it is a duty to recognize my grandfather in the map, like all of those that have come before me, and recognize that my map is not just my own.

It is up to me to craft it; others may study it, some may even profit from it, but using it comes with the knowing caveats that everyone is different, as is each day. Mileage, as they say, may vary . . . mine certainly has. The trick is to always remember everyone that has helped me along and helped me to find my most important path of all—the way home to my valleys, hollows, ridges, and mountains.

Finding one's way is not always easy. For me, it seems to have grown even more difficult as I've gotten older. Twists and turns, blank spots on the map . . . all over the map. Places I've been and long forgotten blur with places I have never been. On that map, places of great vibrance hover next to the tombstones of lost dreams. Still—with the woods and the hills, I look at the ground beneath my feet and the sky showing through the green trees of summer and the barren, dormant trees of winter. Despite it all, I know one thing: this is exactly where I need to be, this spot . . . having found it along this path, this map of my very own.

The Rabbi of Box Turtles

For Dr. Bill Belzer

Bill, at first I mistook you for a Hasid—
Flowing bushy beard, tall, lanky
and—yes, you were a rabbi of sorts,

a Talmudic expert. Like Moses,
they can live up to 120 years but in the wild,
a small parcel of woods where they hatch,

eat slugs, worms, berries, lay their eggs,
biologists like you just beginning
to understand the delicate population

dynamics. You knew they were dying out—
pet collections: *Leave them be*, you repeated,
your mantra, a box turtle yourself,

a self-described "isolate," hiding out
in your corner office on campus,
eating your peanut butter sandwiches.

You knew it was we humans who ruined
them, our penchant to gather and hold onto
and collect, no matter the repercussions.

But it took you to propose the project
of using perpetual radiotelemetric retrieval
to monitor and protect and possibly rebuild

the "extirpated Box Turtle population."
Belzer's Protocol, they called it—signaling
to all the lost through captivity and injury

and habitat destruction that they can be monitored—
radio transmitter attached to their shells—
their movements followed. They can, like children,

be parented. The congregation you nurtured
made certain they didn't wander off too far,
their nests well-leafed, attended to if wounded.

You created an endowment in perpetuity
that would follow the death of the project's
originator—yours, Bill, more than a year ago,

I just learned from a colleague. You told her
not to tell anyone about the brain tumor,
your decision not to pursue treatment: 70,

you made your decision like a scientist
or like Hillel—you understood you are not obliged
to complete the work, but neither are you free

to desist. And so the box turtle commandments
you adhered to and thus wrote down:
Leave it untouched! Behold a life form

that graced this earth before and long after the dinosaurs!
Spread the word to children everywhere—
scout groups, classrooms, bedtime stories!

Naturally, your burial was green.

Fields' Joy

As if cows—for cows were featured in this windfall witnessing—
chose my daughter and my husband separately to know
what most folks never guess. Pat, hiking the Kokosing Trail,
passed a field of cows running, circling, leaping back
and forth in dappling sun, the day not sweltering hot
nor cold, its temperature so in sync with their internal warmth
that it erased their bodies' walls, and they became the field.
Sonya was on a train winding through Pennsylvania
when she lifted her eyes from book to window to see
cows running up a hill and sideways down, tossing horns,
the metronomic brushes of their tails painting air.
Maybe there were moo-songs too, but Pat was too far off,
and Sonya's train was clattering, so cows on mute
were revelators of both fields' inherent joy. They channeled it.
It stirred their hooves to dance. They passed it into pairs
of eyes blue as the sky that domed the cows' cavorting.

Buried Alive (Magicicada)

What will I dig up
today? Do I dare
disturb this earth,
already churned
by children's games,
eager paws, downpours,
freezes and thaws?

Cicadas tunnel and suck
underground for seventeen
years. I know they are there,
beneath the spread of maple
branches and at the base
of the walnut tree, growing.

But what of those who burrowed
into the soft dirt
under the clutch of pines
chopped down last year
and carted away, raw
and broken, the golden
needly earth smeared
with blacktop?

Those cicadas dreaming
of light, climbing to the roof
of their darkness, adolescents
on the move, on a mission
to find a mate of their own.

Buried alive. Trapped.
They're called Magicicada,
and it does seem like magic,
what they do, flourishing
underground, biding their time
to come out and love—

I'm afraid for them, afraid
that all the magic in the world
can't save them from us.

Bird Equations

I haven't done the math,
manipulated those numbers and symbols
of volume, but I make a wild guess
that fifteen bee hummingbirds would fit
inside a human heart.
The numerals of time flit by
so quickly, thrummed away on those wings.
I can't resist them
as they rush away the day.
But when I want to savor a second,
a moment nearly stilled, I wait

with a Great Blue Heron that stands
in listless pools of Standing Stone Creek.
No wind, shadows stop where they fall
as though they could stall the sun.
Rocks touch water
to slow its progress.
And the heron, motionless,
nestles minutes under its feathers.
If my heart hadn't already been broken,
it might have been a sparrow.
It might have been singing all this time.

Karen Whittington Nelson

All the While

Just upstream of the Dillon School Bridge,
the Licking River flows over a mosaic of inlaid shale.
On a slow summer day, I'd pull to the side of the bridge,
leave the engine idling, step to the guardrail to check on the herons.
A few birds were always there, shadows in the middle of the riverbed,
silhouette-thin, a trickle of water ruffling 'round their spindly ankles,
beaks poised, ready to strike any fish floundering in the shallows.
Revving up the truck always set the bridge floor joists shuddering
and the herons startling. Each bird would bark its annoyance and launch,
carrying the memory of water skyward on broad, undulating wings
that broke like gray waves against the parched clouds.

Maybe one of these days, you and me could drive on over there?
I'll show you where I hoisted you up onto the guardrail that time
so you'd see the herons. We watched 'em take to the sky
and disappear into a puckered bank of sullen clouds.
You covered your ears and squealed with laughter when the clouds
cracked open with thunder. But when the neon lightning sizzled
and serrated the sky with the sign of Zorro, and the green riverbanks
glowed with the eerie yellow of a porch bug light—I grabbed your hand
and we ran like hell for the shelter of the truck, all the while
the summer sky washing down upon us in fine, gray-feathered sheets.

Chuck Salmons

At the Dawn of the Anthropocene

at Ferncliff Peninsula National Natural Landmark,
Ohiopyle, PA, dedicated 1973

The trail winds beneath hemlock, magnolia,
through an ocean of ferns. Rhododendron
blossoms echo the Youghiogheny whitewater
meandering through the Laurel Highlands.
Yellow blazes march us among plants out of place,
their seeds brought northward by the river
from Maryland and West Virginia like immigrants
into this acclimatized gorge whose thickened warmth
trickles down our spines and soaks our shirts
in July heat hazed by wildfire smoke.

We trek past moss-strewn sandstone
outcrops stamped with scaley traces
of *Lepidodendron* and fossil roots,
giant trees lost to deep Earth time.
We pass trunks of American Beech, bark
once smooth now etched by humans who
give little thought to health and less to history.
Ahead, a young couple stops along the trail,
the woman, her face without wrinkles,
keeps lookout as her partner carves their initials,
his hand guided by hubris. We pass them,
say nothing, offer a simple look in the eye
more of disappointment than disdain.

Further along we see an area fenced off.
Its sign explains how restoration is at work,
how the deer gorged themselves,
rendered the zone fruitless. We speak
softly about the Dust Bowl and deforestation,
mountain-top mines, nuclear testing.
How a few hundred miles north in Ontario,
our everlasting mark on the planet is revealed
in lake sediments tainted with atomic evidence.
We wonder, where are the fences for the beeches?
Who will tame us? Millennia from now,
who will unearth and collect our fallen remains
locked in bedrock, our identities imprinted
like so many limbs of an extinct species?

No One Had to Tell Me

Most workday evenings, my father would pass morsels of incidents around the dinner table that had occurred as he completed various dirty and dangerous jobs. Never having been inside a factory, I had trouble imagining the reality of it all. The time clock stealing away the hours as Dad inched toward disabled sprinklers hanging from the factory ceiling; he and the sprinklers both suspended by a few bolts and belts as he made repairs. Machinery, running full tilt on the sawdust-strewn floor, screaming a hole through the stifling air, leaving him temporarily immune to other sounds.

Mom would stop clearing the table, touch his shoulder, put her other hand to her mouth, her dish towel scrunched into her palm, forgotten. I'd anchor his stories to something relatable, imagine Dad an acrobat, dazzling the workers below as he soared from rafter to rafter.

He sometimes mentioned by name someone he'd seen below on the factory floor— occasionally it was a neighbor lady whose kid my sister and I knew from school. If a woman working below happened to look up and see him, she'd nudge the woman sitting next to her. Before you knew it, a surge of upturned faces, feminine smiles and waving arms sweep along the assembly line. Dad laughed, said that kind of thing ate up the hours and made his day.

When my little sister, Susie, and I were excused from the table to watch cartoons in the front room, Dad's stories became less humorous and sometimes scary. Eavesdropping, I heard him tell Mom that often those same women, struggling to meet quota and intent on clocking out at the end of their shift with all their fingers, had not even noticed him up there. He said those gals worked the line with a vengeance. I tried to picture it— all those ladies, unaware of my father laboring in the rafters, holding his wrench with a death grip above their hair-netted heads.

Now I know that eight hours of snaking on his stomach through crawl spaces twenty-some feet above the factory floor with a toolbelt of wrenches clawing at his belly, breathing in industrialized dust and the filth of pigeon droppings, would have taken everything my young sturdy father had clocked in with most mornings.

At the end of a shift on a hot summer day, he'd clock out and return to the treeless back lot where our old car, Betsy, sat baking like a forgotten tater in an oven. Dad would roll down her windows before gingerly sliding across the vinyl seat—no doubt keeping his work gloves on as a buffer between his hands and the scorching steering wheel. Instead of relief, his body sometimes gave unwelcomed hints of what was to come as he drove the seven miles home.

I remember such a day; Susie and I waiting on the front porch as we did most summer afternoons. Seeing the car come up the lane, we jumped from the porch, laughing and yelling, "Daddy's home!"

We ran alongside the car and jumped away from the lumpy tires as they rolled to a stop in the driveway. And believe me, no one had to tell me to wipe the smile from my face once I jerked open the rusty door handle of the old Plymouth and came eye to eye with my father. I recognized the situation immediately and quickly sobered up, looked over my shoulder and gave Susie the *look*. She got big-eyed and quiet.

Dad sat straight-backed against the ripped, vinyl seat, a mist of clammy sweat clinging to his face. He had a gritty set to his jaw and his dark eyes were red-rimmed, steel marbles. He saved that face for only two occasions, to hold back a whole lot of pain, or to let somebody know you'd best back off if you knew what was good for you. I wasn't scared; Daddy never pulled that tough guy face on me.

Without dislodging his left forearm from its location on his thigh, he bent back his wrist, cupped his fingers and made a slight wave in the direction of our house. I was still nodding my understanding as Susie and I raced each other to the house shouting, "Mom! Daddy's throwed his back out again!"

Even then, I knew there was no real need to alert Mom; she didn't miss much and this was not a novel problem. But our family had our rituals and we each played our part.

Mom knew when to expect Dad home from work and she'd been listening for the car as she put dinner on. Hearing the crunch of gravel in the lane, she ran to the kitchen window. She suspected what was wrong when she saw the car limping slowly into the driveway. Mom always said Old Betsy knew when Daddy needed to be handled gently and would coddle him like an egg if need be.

Mom tossed her dish towel over a chair back, rummaged through the cabinets for the aspirin, filled a Tupperware tumbler with tap water and rushed toward the back door.

Susie and I met Mom just as she flung open the screen door. We jumped out of her way. She wasn't stopping and she was bigger than us. Besides, Dad needed her.

Mom ran to the car, jerked open the door and handed the open aspirin bottle to Dad.

He shook out a palmful of the chalky disks, downed them with the water, grimaced and leaned back to wait for relief.

Mom shooed Susie and me away and climbed into the passenger seat to offer him some comfort. She always sat with Dad in the car when he came home like this, because, as she'd told me once when a tearful Aunt Mary had come for an unannounced visit without Uncle Bob—misery loves company.

We retreated to the porch and perched on the steps. Susie sidled up close to me as we hugged our knees and worried.

Mom leaned toward Daddy so he'd not have to turn to see her.

I watched her through the car window; her mouth moved, but I could not unscramble the silent words. It reminded me of watching Mrs. Cleaver lecture the Beaver on a mute TV, our show interrupted by the rare evening phone call.

Half an hour later, Dad began the slow, agonizing journey from car to house. He made it inside as far as the recliner. Susie and I unlaced his heavy work boots and pulled off his sweaty socks as he reminded us, "Easy, girls. Easy!" He told us not to be silly because it hurt when we made him laugh, but he smiled as we giggled and held our noses.

Susie and I ate supper at the kitchen table; Mom was too busy to eat. When we finished, she allowed us to sit on the floor and watch TV with Dad until bedtime.

Dad spent the evening nibbling baloney on crackers and sipping canned soup. When he pulled the aspirin bottle from the pocket of his t-shirt and downed more aspirin, Mom looked at the clock and I knew she wanted to say something. He winked at us and patted Mom's arm and told her not to worry, everything would be all right. She fed him hot soup from a spoon and cooed to him like he was a baby bird.

Dad was up before the sun the next morning. My twin bed was closer to our bedroom door and I woke up when he switched on the bare-bulb hall light. I watched from my bed as Dad and his shadow passed by, stumbling toward the bathroom, pausing every few steps to lean against the wall. I suddenly felt hot, and something new and nameless made my heart lurch. I almost called out to him but changed my mind just in time. It didn't feel right for my father to know that I'd seen him like that. I rolled over and fell back to sleep.

This is as far as memory takes me, but I'll round out the events that I was not actually privy to, fill in the cracks until I am satisfied with the ending that I've pieced together. I imagine my father an hour or so past the moment when I'd seen him in the hallway.

Now, on the other side of town, he carefully picks a path across the factory's heavily graveled parking lot. He slows every few steps, sips steaming black coffee from his metal thermos, and nods to quiet, shadowy men emerging from the fog. All of them crunch toward the brick building with the same determined look.

Once inside, he stands stiffly before the time clock. Anxious to start the day, he punches in a few minutes early and heads toward the tool room, his stiff gait and slight stumble barely noticeable.

He wastes no time collecting the tools needed for the day's job; he's on the clock. But as he buckles his toolbelt securely around his waist he thinks of us: Mom folding laundry on the kitchen table as she drinks her coffee and plans her day. Susie and me, safe, still asleep upstairs.

Dad begins his rounds, already counting down the hours until he is back home where he belongs—with us. I know without a doubt, this ending rings true.

It's Not the Sound

It's not the sound of a human voice, though husky, nor harmony,
though it shrills the harmonic compression of one long note.

It is the voice of a shovel singing before its labor, clearing a path
in the night with a hum, a sigh, a wail of *why,* a dirge denying defeat.

Its elongated throat-clearing sound croons us to sleep inside the
    erasure
of light, declaring the trial over, the jury swayed to mercy by its

prolonged peroration. We live a block from these passing trains,
open beds of coal winking like glittering sightless eyes, graffitied
    tankers

surging with the insouciance of youth. There's one soul and one
    soul only
on board, folded into the conductor who may or may not
    acknowledge

my fluttering red-gloved hand. Speed begets distance, evanescence,
a keening beyond the reveries of rabbits, owls, deer, fomenting
    flowers,

the fortune in pennies flattened on rails. A strap pull doles out
    duration,
converting far to near, to a song with the timbre of a tiger

swallowing his sinews and paws while churning our dreams
with the zone's vegetation in the heat of his belly's broth.

Not quite blues nor mantra nor banshee's scream, this alto-
baritone refrain suggests the sound of gravel pulverized to sand.

On Finding Out My Bastard-Father's Half-brothers and Half-sisters Were Protective of Him as a Child in Kentucky

It doesn't explain his hatred for his father. The clenched jaw
he'd wear whenever he talked about Bob Beach. Or a tear—

whisperings may have been news of the father who limped
because it only takes once to say far too much to some men.

It didn't make much difference who brought it up; he just
declined to hear it mentioned, even without judgment or

condescension. He'd flip out if we broached the subject.
He's ten years dead and well-buried when I hear that his

half-brothers and -sisters looked out for him growing up.
That they put movie money in his small hand at the Neon

or motioned to the usher to let him through without paying—
pictures like *Wild West Days* with Johnny Mack Brown whose

tin-star sheriff had Kentucky in his name. A talent for gunplay.
I know now there is a private linguistics to sorrow and shame.

He wasn't the homeliest boy in Fleming-Neon grade school,
my father, and no one picked on him without answering for it,

so the archeology of his life wasn't unearthed by me or anyone.
I don't speak Bastard or Hillbilly, but when he spoke I listened—

in neon-lit darknesses or on the streets of small Kentucky towns
wherein our American language fights not to fail us but then does.

Often, he said it wasn't any of our goddamn business. The protocol:
every spigot of memory opened was his to close without explanation.

Summer in Greenfield

I

when the kids got bored
with throwing bricks at buses
they would come down off the hill
to stand in the mist
floating from the carwash

II

opening the windows
meant inviting in a random cloud
of trash pile odor into your kitchen
because the college students
across the street didn't understand
taking out the trash
meant it had to be in a bag or a can
that you dragged to the curb
on a special day of the week
they thought it just had to be outside
and the trash collector did the rest

III

waking up every morning
wondering if anyone I encounter
will decide they want
to get in a fistfight today

IV

nights on the front porch
trying to stay cool
drinking lemonade
watching the streetlights
keeping a baseball bat
tucked away nearby
just in case

V

sweeping broken glass
off the sidewalk
every morning
on the weekends

VI

late August, early September
the heroin pipeline into Pittsburgh
goes dry
once you learn this
suddenly, everything
about everyone around
makes a lot more sense

Linda Mills Woolsey

Sunday Drive in the Sixties

From the car radio, Cash and Cline sing heartbreak.
Our old Buick's name is Edna and her engine purrs
with American know-how. Between our skirmishes

in the backseat, we count cows—if we pass a cemetery
on your side, you have to bury them all. It's a game—
we can always start over. Dad drives the long way round

so we can stop for gas at a place that keeps a black bear
chained out back. There, Dad buys colas for us all—even
the bear. As the beast guzzles sweet poison, pop trickles

down over his leather muzzle onto rusty fur. The stink
of his wildness is worse than the town dump in August
and he wears a halo of flies. They crawl on the rims

of eyes that glare at me as we drive away. From the radio
a man's voice assures us that we're still testing the A-bomb—
though we know it works. In Georgia, the state police are

cracking down on troublemakers. In Algeria—wherever
that is—there's been a "massacre." I sound out the syllables
so I can look the word up later. Then we pass a house where

the lanterns' kerosene glow haloes faces of bearded men,
and sturdy women wearing neat white caps. The light is so gentle
it kisses the wings of a thousand moths as they flutter up

with something like hope. Switching off the radio, Dad whispers,
"Look!" We do. He turns at the next farm, drives back slowly,
decorously, as if our car has joined a funeral procession,

without the death. "Look," he urges us again, "that's what peace
looks like." I memorize a line of chairs, a chiaroscuro glimpse
of lamplit faces. They ride with me as the body count begins,

as mills and mines fail, as a muzzled rage dogs us all down
the years as they carry us far from the sabbath island of that calm.

At the Corner of Tunstall St.

there is a triangle shaped house
wedged at the bottom of
a street so steep, the sidewalks
are stairs, and in that house once lived
an old man who, when it got warm,
would watch his living room TV while sitting
on a folding chair on his stoop, wearing
only swim trunks, holding
the screen door open, sticking
his head inside the house so he could see

When I Was You

There were four of us in the car—Bethel, her husband Levi, Bethel's brother Cyril, and me. Bethel and I were nearly the same age, but even though we had grown up less than a mile from one another in the already small town of Harleysville, we knew each other only in passing, having crossed paths at youth group socials or the Apple Butter Frolic. About a year ago, we bumped into each other at a farmer's market in the East End of Pittsburgh and realized that we were once again living a few blocks from one another, three hundred miles from home. Hey, we said, if we're ever going back east at the same time, we should carpool. And, that's what had put me there in that car with them. I had gone home for my aunt's funeral; Bethel and the others, for her older sister's baby shower.

One hardly imagines dying in the company of loose acquaintances with whom one is splitting gas and tolls. But so it was.

We were still two hours from Pittsburgh when Bethel saw this little spot off the side of the road—a long-grassed meadow and a spectacular view—and asked Levi to pull off. It was a nice place to get out and let the scenery stop moving for a few minutes. He parked the car between the rocky overlook and a wild apple tree, its branches knobbed with ripe green fruit.

Everyone got out. Beyond the apple tree, Cyril discovered a little foot path that dipped across a creek and meandered up a hill on the opposite side—but he had ventured too far for Bethel's comfort, and she was going after him to call him back. Levi was eyeing the apple tree, perhaps debating whether he could harvest some of its apples. I lingered awkwardly by the car, one of those compact SUVs that can't make up its mind whether it is a sedan or a truck.

I didn't want to be the one to hold us up when it was time to leave, so I hung close to the vehicle, doing half-hearted lunges and worrying about whether I would have time to do a load of laundry tonight when I got home. And so I gave away the final moments of my life, in ignorance that they were the last, to meaningless fretting.

I was using the back bumper to brace my calf stretches when the car began to roll forward very slightly. Mortified, I hooked my fingers under the bumper and leaned back against the car's drift. The edge of the plastic cut into my knuckles, but I held on, glancing nervously over at Levi. I didn't want him to think that I was messing with his car. But his attention was still with the apple tree. Despite the anchor of my body, the heavy vehicle crunched forward stubbornly. I scrambled to the front to try another tack.

I planted my feet, hands on either side of the sleek little emblem on the grille, and pushed, but the weight of the car, now gathering a bit of momentum, edged me back. My all-consuming thought—one of the last that I could call my own—was that Levi would turn away from that apple tree and realize what was happening. Some random-ass person his wife barely knew tagging along on their family trip and screwing with his car. I stepped back to gain a bit of leverage, and my foot hit air.

I gasped at the missed step, just sucked air and fell backwards over the drop-off, too suddenly to cry out. The car kept rolling after me, its front wheels dropping over the edge, the undercarriage hitting rock and dirt and knocking a chunk of the cliff face loose; the earth crumbled away, and a wisp of clay-brown dust curled out where it separated from the sheer wall. I was falling, and this huge machine, riding on a shower of dirt and rocks, was falling after me. The slow, cold passage of the end of time.

I watched the lip of the cliff scroll up over the sight of Levi under the apple tree—tall, wearing thick glasses, his hands braced on his back, neck craned up at the fruit among the leaves and crooked limbs—and I desperately did not want to lose that sight. I reached for him. I flung myself at him and then—fleetingly—into him. I entered and left him in a single moment. But in that space of no time at all, I knew him.

The muscles of his abdomen were tight from leaning back.

The hairs of his legs just faintly brushed against his khaki pants.

His steady consciousness lingered on the tree, though the sound of the car hitting the cliff's edge had just now caught his ear and was beginning to claim some part of his thoughts.

He had been wondering—was still wondering—what it was like to exist as a tree. He had given himself roots and branches in mirror-image canopies, and he was considering the feel of the sun on his leaves.

As a tree, he stood in constant but incremental motion for seasons, years. Not at all like graduate school, all deadlines and results. What was the point, really? The world being what it was, how many more white men with master's degrees in computer science were actually required? That sounded like something Cyril would say. Cyril. Now, that's integrity. Dumpster diving; biking everywhere, even in the freaking snow. Brave, too. He had done illegal shit, chaining himself to a pipeline. Spent a week in jail and was still paying off that fine. Levi hadn't even thought of putting his own hands into that sawed off PVC cuff. The angry workers, the angry cops, they scared him. What must Cyril think of him?

Levi had plans to do something that mattered. Applying machine learning to identify bias in juvenile sentencing. Or a program to map air monitoring information onto wind patterns, pinpointing major sources of pollution. But he hadn't done those things yet. So when would he? Or would he be satisfied with a job at Google so long as his uncles laid off him about how much money he made? Still, nothing he had done (nothing he could ever do) amounted to one iota of what the tree gave to this world. How much better, to be an apple tree. If he were an apple tree, then Bethel would be . . .

Bethel. I flashed through his hands against his back, the little soreness in his shoulders from driving, the hunger tugging at his gut, but she was almost all of his mind now. If he were a tree, then she would be the sun, the groundwater. Absorbable, apart. She was the network of fungus in the soil, trading sweetness with him in easy partnership: her galloping laugh, her sarcasm, her big front teeth, her soft places, her callouses. She was there in the periphery of his sight. In the instant before he looked towards the falling car, his attention strung out towards the little blur of her as she followed after her brother.

I ran along the thread of his attention like electricity, and then I was with her.

She was hungry too, but also nauseous. From the car ride? Or.

She had broken a sweat, tromping after Cyril, and the stir of the breeze cooled the fine, damp, nut-brown curls at her neck as I entered.

Her body was in motion, feeling the pleasure of its own strength and activity after being so long cooped up in the car. She sensed Levi's eyes on her. And it made her skin radiate. The way he was so aware of her all the time: he made her feel extraordinarily real. The matter of her body seemed more tangible because he was thinking about her, holding her in his mind. Since she was eleven years old and Alicia Hagey had pulled her aside after gym class to suggest that she should try to spend as little time as possible with her shirt off to hide her pudgy stomach, Bethel had willed her body to be imperceptible.

And then Levi. How he had so curiously, so assiduously, perceived her. How he had brushed his cheek against her open thighs, eyes closed. How he had tracked every line of her with utter focus. She had become as solid as rock. The first time he had touched her like that, he had anchored her. And every time since. Every time.

It was stupid, careless, to leave her visibility, her permanence, up to him. Why hadn't she been able to anchor herself without him? Stupid, though, to resent him for it. But if. If it were true. She couldn't bear the thought that his focus might drift from her. Would the life that was—might be—growing inside her distract him? Would he attend less to her body for the body she held? What if the work of loving herself was still undone, and this baby—if there was a baby—revealed to the whole world how unprepared she was?

A baby. A curl of life-to-be. Bethel became aware of her own strength. Her beating heart. Her organs, flush with vitality. She would be rear-ranged to accommodate another body. Push it out. Levi with a sleeping infant on his chest, its pink lips barely parted. Picky eating and night-mares and family jokes and, *Tell me a story about when I was baby*. To see her body echoed in another body. Would her child learn from her how to shrink and be unseen, how to reject their own body? And what if she lost the pregnancy? Bethel ached and eased at the thought. She imagined them on this trail together, Levi holding one hand, she the other, and *one-two-three-whee!* Ahead on the trail, Uncle Cyril watching something in the dirt—an ant dragging the crumpled body of a spider. Cyril, calling to the child to come see.

Cyril had been so sweet at the shower, exclaiming over the tiny booties. She felt a little gloat of joy. That she would have him close. That he would belong to her child just a little more than to its cousin. Her beautiful, tender, odd, good-hearted, courageous brother who worried her and needed her and whom she needed.

Cyril had turned back on the trail and was waiting for his sister. His face, like his shoulders, small and square; shaggy, sandy hair half-lifted in a breeze. The line that connected Bethel to Cyril was not taut but soft, like a wide satin ribbon, and I followed the tie between them driftingly. Hanging between them on the ribbon of love, I contemplated him. Boyish. Youth was persistent in him. Yet he was old, too, somehow. Ancient. He looked like a statue, standing there, one leg up on a rock, arm cocked on his knee, head turned towards the horizon—a visionary in cargo shorts and skater shoes, gauges in his ears. And then I was with him.

His skin prickled with sweat, itchy.

The sun glared, making him squint.

And his thoughts were of Bethel. Mothering sister coming after him. His heart heated with affection and anger at the way she cared so much. Owned him, almost. Maybe he should move. He had never lived anywhere on his own. Always tagging along, little brother. Getting into trouble. But leaving was bone-hollow loneliness. He didn't want to be so far that he couldn't just show up at his sister's house, kicked back on the porch swing when she got home so that she would laugh and ask, *How long have you been here?* and he would shrug and dismount the swing and come inside and follow her around and talk about whatever. Levi, too. It made him want to cry, how Levi loved Bethel. It made him want to kiss Levi right on the forehead and put a ring of gold on his head, like some medieval king distributing his blessings.

Not like Levi needed his approval. So fucking smart. Golden boy. But not, somehow, an asshole. No doubt Levi thought *he* was a loser—barely employed, no car. A criminal. What good had that done? They built the pipeline anyway. When was he going to grow up already?

Was that supposed to happen already? When had Bethel stopped being a kid with him? Cyril missed being kids together. He missed not having to guess when to go home so his sister could be alone with her husband. And he, alone-alone because it was just him in his alone, whereas their alone was Bethel-and-Levi. And then Bethel-and-Levi-and-kiddo, eventually. She had been weird at the baby shower. He wondered, was she already pregnant? Would she stop mothering him when she had a real kid?

Babies made him want to cry, too. Their eldest sister, all round and tired and determined, made him want to cry. One month, and he would be an uncle. A little girl, they said. But the name was still a secret. They should stick with that, let her live her life with a secret name.

Everyone does anyway. Bethel and Levi had secret names. Could he guess them? What about that person who was driving with them this weekend? He couldn't even remember her actual name. But what did that matter? Her real name was an unknowable secret. And so was his, but he couldn't think of it.

A secret from oneself. At his parents' house this weekend, sitting on his old blue-green plaid bedspread, he had read straight through one of his old high school journals. And he had not recognized himself. He remembered almost nothing in the journal. He had written out a prayer for an audition, for a part he didn't get. One entry wrote down the inanities of baseball practice, and then there were these long passages about Joan of Arc and the Spanish Inquisition and the Exorcist. Nothing familiar, nothing that mattered. Whatever his name was back then, that name had been erased. From that strange child, someone else—but it could have been a hundred different someone elses.

And now? Cyril could feel his name changing already. Ahead, there was yet another someone else (or an array of them, a crowd of strangers), inevitable. No. Not inevitable. Anything but certain. It could all end in a second. *Like it did for you, right?*

I was shocked to realize he meant me.

He had seen it happen. Through his eyes, behind Bethel and beyond Levi, I saw the falling, fallen car. I had already disappeared below the cliff's edge, already flown. But he wasn't speaking to me out there, over the edge of the cliff. He was speaking to me now, clinging to the life inside of him. The twoness of us began to roil, struggle, sorting out what parts were him and which were me. I remembered his boyhood and felt the slick of his armpits, and he was knotted in my longing to still be breathing, my frantic rehearsal of all I meant to do tonight and tomorrow and the rest of my life that was not my life anymore. Laundry, love, a trip to see the Pacific. All of a sudden, he got free of me and pulled away, but he did not release me. He held me and pressed his question to me again, *Did you know the end was coming?*

I didn't. I vibrated with how much I did not know, with the shock of my death.

He made himself a hedge around me to keep me there. *Were you with the others, too? Levi and Bethel?*

Yes. Briefly.

And?

They love you.

His consciousness flexed at this, like a lung expanding, and the pressure around me changed, giving me a giddy sense of growth. *Did you learn their secret names?*

Yes. Partly.

And?

I can't tell you.

Can't or . . .

I have forgotten them. I am forgetting it all now. One was a tree, I think. The other, a heart? . . . legs and bones? I don't remember.

Will you stay with me?

I think so. I am with you now. What else is there?

He showed me what else there was, and I wept.

It's gone, isn't it? My life is gone

Deepening the walls of himself, he comforted me. *Yes. I'm sorry. It's okay. It's okay, now. That's all in the past. And now . . .*

Now you are with me.

Now I am with you.

He and I grew still together.

Now is almost gone, too. It will be over soon.

Where will I go then?

He thought about it, and I trickled out along the gesture of his thought. I twined out from him, an arching, twisting line. As soon as I was free of his perimeter, I pulled towards the domed sky with urgency, but something snagged. A filament, running through Cyril, through Bethel, through Levi, over the edge of the cliff to my fallen body. I was caught. The line of me began to contract, coiling up like a piece of yarn when one of the fibers is pulled. My snagged spirit snarled, its fibers packing denser and denser, compressing and fusing, until I was a tight seed of being, ovoid and smooth, and I hung there on the thread like a kite.

Forearm struck rock, a scraping of flesh from bone that shivered through the line. Back against a toppled trunk, the force of it cracking the spine. Head jarred out of place by a branch. In a shower of crumbled glass and dirt, the metal bulk of the car crushing legs, ribs, skull.

The thread snapped.

Unbound, the hard seed of me lifted, flew. Below, the dust of the collapsed cliffside plumed out, and little figures ran towards it. Then they were too small, and it was lines of roads through green trees, the first brushes of autumn in their leaves and crusted patches of square buildings and parking lots. Then texture on a bent horizon, then a planet, then beyond, and I turned to watch the approach.

Elizabeth McConnell

Ready for Flight

Up against the green rushes, she stands,
slate gray, still as a headstone.
On the water, her cloudlike reflection
faces a bright and cloudless sky.

Stalking Great Blue Heron at the pond.
One foot always in front of the other.
Ready to strike and
ready for flight.

Securing no camouflage
she will stay along the edges,
weave among the milkweeds,
steps splaying flat and wide.

All day she can wait, wade and feed
until finally and completely sated
following the crush and crunch of crayfish,
bountiful swallows of fleshy bullfrogs.

From across the pond
I lower my binoculars.
Release them from ringless fingers,
meeting no one halfway.

What became of the wasp

that got away from nest I smashed
with the butt of my hoe? I never saw

it buzz off toward the field. So, hoe
in hand I walk to the garden draped

green and rowed with seedling corn.
Pigweed carpets the space between

the crops' sprouted leaves and the fence
meant to stave off deer who survived the hunt

and hunger season, the bucks and does
who covet what I grow. I power down

the hot-wire strands, stand with my
feet planted wide and hack

through what's grown between me
and sinking my teeth into summer

sweet—when I hear behind me
a saw-toothed buzz and turn and see

an antlered hornet, or is it a buck
with stinger, curled and venom-tipped

bent towards me? An incubus, a peryton
of bilious dreams rises like a djinni

over me, holding, it seems, an oak trunk
in its djinni-limbs. It turns and banshee-buzzes

a straight way toward my home, my nest
where all my children are still at rest.

Ephemeron

I sit with my thoughts and bourbon
these long evenings
      dipping day into dark

when edges of the woods creep closer,
      but no one notices,
            and the birds, frogs, and salamanders
      all mate in our yards.

They cry out songs of love and loneliness.
The chill coming down from the mountains

pokes goosebumps out all across my skin
      while I listen and wait
            for lightning bugs to rise up off the creek banks.

I wonder if this is how life is supposed to be,
      fueled by hot desire,
            peaking in sunshine, and then

this desolate hour seeping into our mortality and

      waiting for the end.

After Grief

He had not been thrown
    out of life but out
of the country of marriage
    to live in a trailer
in the woods, plywood
    hovel of penance
haunted by vipers and skunks.
    He had failed to attend to
feelings, bull-running his way
    through marriage, through works and days,
wrecking silence, peace, time.

    Failure is always noisy,
however hidden—the
    slate-fall in the dark-hearted mine
of self, the warning canary
    choked and crushed. Still,
fragments of goodness may remain, small survivals
    like minnows in a drying stream,
or a high hawk's nest at the edge
    of the burning strip mine.
Ah, holy bafflement and grace.
    Ah, second chances after landslide
and flood. Ah, mercy given freely,
    a hover of glad glinting midges
over the slump of a grave.

Powerline

Summer, 1975

"Snake, snake," Uncle Glen yells, and we all scatter down the Powerline, hanging onto our buckets of blackberries as we run. It's a red-hot day in July, and the sweat pours over my dirty, ten-year-old face as I hustle over to my mother, my legs hot and itchy in blue jeans and thick socks. My family and I wait for Glen to give the OK to come back up the hill. "It's gone," he finally calls, and we gingerly walk back up the hill, keeping an eye out for additional snakes as we go. "Ugh, I hate snakes," my mom says and shudders. My uncle laughs again, looking around a second time to make sure no other snakes are lurking around waiting for a bite.

"That was a big old copperhead," my Uncle Glen laughs. "I almost stepped on him, he was so close. We musta caught him sleeping in the sun."

Nothing in these southern Ohio woods scares Uncle Glen. He's been hunting mushrooms and ginseng in them since he was twelve years old. He makes a lot of money selling his ginseng every year, and you never see him driving his old car to town without a few bunches of it drying in the backseat window.

Glen is a tall, thin man with a headful of wavy black hair and a stooped-over walk. He has never been to school and cannot read or write because he was born with severe congenital heart and lung defects. He couldn't walk by himself until he was eleven years old. That was the year grandma and grandpa took him to Columbus for a newly developed, experimental operation that by some miracle he survived. After the surgery, physical therapists helped him develop the strength to stand up and walk the hospital corridors. Mom says that when her brother finally came home from the hospital, the first thing he did was jump out of the car and swing from the branch of a big oak tree standing out in the yard. He swung from the branch, yelling at his brothers and sisters, "Look at me!"

He was just that happy to finally be able to walk and play. Until then, grandma had packed Glen everywhere he needed to go. My uncle has never forgotten that, either. He still loves my crotchety grandma better than anyone else in the world, even better than his wife and children.

Uncle Glen sees his doctors for checkups every year, and every time they tell him he's only

got a few more years to live. They've been telling him this for almost thirty years. Glen just laughs and keeps hunting the Tar Hollow Forest that he knows so well. Today, he hunts blackberries, tomorrow, mayapple or perhaps more ginseng. Whatever Glen gathers in Tar Hollow, he'll either fashion into the powerfully good pies that my grandma taught him to make—or sell for a tidy profit.

Looking back, I don't know for sure why that stretch of land out in the Tar Hollow woods is called the Powerline, but I suspect there must be (or at one time must have been) some kind of electrical grid out there, and for all I know, still is. I haven't been back to that beautiful, isolated spot in years, but I can still see the bushes upon bushes of blackberries that grew, at least back then, along the top of the Powerline. Every summer, my family, my Uncle Glen, and my Uncle Wendell would drive out there to pick them in the blistering hot sun, sweltering in our long-sleeved shirts and jeans. We had to wear them to keep from getting scratched by brambles or stung by bees. However, our protective clothing gave us little-to-no defense against snakes.

But, to return to that red-hot day in 1975, while I certainly don't want to run into snakes on any day of the week, my ten-year-old self hates picking blackberries even more than the thought of stepping on slithery reptiles. I can never pick them as fast as my nine-year-old sister Cheryl, and even worse, for every berry I pick, I squash two. I can pluck at blackberries forever, it seems like, only to look down and discover that my bucket looks almost empty. My mom and dad, though, effortlessly pick quart buckets full of blackberries. One brush of their hands along blackberry brambles sends fruit plumping into their buckets. The heat doesn't seem to bother them, either, although surely it must. No trees provide shade along the flat top of that broad hill, so the sun beats down without mercy. Unlike me, though, mom and dad never complain, just keep picking. Nothing pierces their calm complacency—except for snakes.

Yet the thought of Glen's blackberry pies makes the hot sun, the snakes, the bee stings, and my overall sweaty misery almost worth the Powerline trip. My mom makes blackberry pies, too, delicious double-crusted pies with sweet, buttery juice oozing from them. She also makes blackberry jam and blackberry dumplings. She cans some of the blackberries for winter, too, and when she does, the kitchen smells hot, steamy, and delicious. When she cooks mustard greens and dandelion greens, however, I try to stay far, far away from the kitchen. Blackberries smell much better than boiling mustard greens—mustard greens smell like dirt and make my eyes sting. However, I like to pick greens much better than blackberries even though I have to stoop a lot to dig them out of the earth. It's easy to fill up a big bag with dandelion greens. Dandelions grow everywhere in the springtime. Of course, greens aren't the only vegetables that my family eats, we grow a garden full of beans and potatoes, but they're certainly the cheapest ones—free and easily available to anyone who cares to pick them.

Free—just like sweet, delicious blackberries and the green-jacketed walnuts falling off black walnut trees all over the southern Ohio countryside. And unlike blackberries, I like to pick walnuts under those cool, shady trees and then toss them into white, five-gallon buckets. It's so much fun to fill the buckets, but strangely enough, my sister hates picking walnuts almost as much as I hate picking blackberries. However, we both love the walnut-studded fudge that our mom makes with them.

Of course, we all love blackberry pie, too, so even though my pretty young mom is deathly afraid of snakes, she doesn't ask dad to quit picking blackberries on that blistering day. She just keeps picking them throughout that hot, humid afternoon. My nineteen-year-old Uncle Wendell picks beside her, quiet as always, his long, 1970s-style brown hair lank and sweaty in the sun. He would rather be fishing, of course; Wendell loves to fish, but he still lives with grandma and grandpa and knows how much grandma wants some blackberries to can. So, he picks, although

I suspect that Wendell, like me, would rather be doing something else. There's just something about the set of his shoulders as he trudges from bush to bush. I know that he hates roasting temperatures as much as I do, even more, ever since he nearly died from heat stroke, mowing Jones Cemetery out in ninety-degree weather.

Yet we continue to pick until late afternoon. Finally, though, my dad speaks up and says that he's beat, and it's time to pack up and go. My uncles agree, and we begin the long trek down the Powerline to the waiting cars. My little brother walks beside dad, eager in his little-boy way to help load the buckets inside the car. Like he does everything, my dad efficiently packs the berries away in the trunk. Dad takes time to look around before we leave, though, breathing everything in before getting behind the wheel. I know what he's feeling because I feel it too. A powerful stillness exists out here in these woods, a stillness sweet enough to make me cry. While it will be good to get back on the road and make our way home, a part of me wishes we could stay, pitch a tent, and camp out here for a while. Just listen to all that silence, eat the blackberries we picked together, and forget, at least for a while, about the things that matter outside the Powerline.

Tom Donlon

Sandy, Golden Lab

for the Demeys

She goes down tomorrow, the day
she turns sweet sixteen. She is blind,
incontinent, won't eat much, pees
when it storms, gets carried upstairs.

Husband and wife decide tonight
if it is right to put her down, to keep
an appointment with the vet, to visit
on her the irreversible, the long sleep.

At the pool party for the girls' soccer team,
Sandy presses the probe of her golden nose
under my arm toward my fried chicken.
Two jade buttons for eyes look at me.

She is cordial, yet follows the smell,
single-minded and firm. I discourage this
in my own dog, but Sandy is short on time,
and I know too much. Because I linger,

Sandy edges along the table, her frame
greyhound thin, in part from heritage
(what mysteries lie in our lineage),
in part from dog years I did not calculate.

Her legs stutter and weave on narrow hips,
yet she moves on, avid for breath, enjoys,
through the cataract of her life, the surprises
and pulls fruit from branches she can reach.

Night Fishing on French Creek

for K.L. Lockhart (1907-1987)

Silence was the price of being with you
in the star-splashed and forbidden dark.
So I sat small in the prow and stiff
as a figurehead, facing you while
you rowed out from cottage lamps
into the tree-hung dark.

You baited your hook without a word
as the black creek slapped the hull
and bullfrogs sang, "too deep, too deep."
Loose-tongued moonlight babbled
on the water—one more unruly child
scaring the fish away.

When the moon and I held our tongues
and the night was black-dark, sufficient,
your line bent to invisible forces
as my cat's-eyes caught the knot
of your muscles reeling in the world
through a crease in the water.

Strong hand on mine, you cursed the fish
aboard. A dark slash of life spilled from
the loop of our rough net to writhe
solid and wet on the wood at my feet—
her gill-slits pulsing silver, white mouth
opening, closing without a word.

Even by daylight I bit my tongue
as your pistol shouted over the water.
You taught me to hear the kingfishers
cry "Christ, Christ, Christ it's hot!"
their voices echoing down the creek
with your double-barreled laughter.

Some nights you still charm me away
from the screened-in world of sleep,
where Nana plays solitaire, slapping
cards on blue and white enamel as moths
circle the light, bent on the death
you aimed to keep at bay forever.

Train Ride

Northern Central tracks zipper
the hollows of Pennsylvania hills

blurring through steam locomotive
smoke swirling with my thoughts

of Gettysburg and my brother who
was killed there thirty years ago.

Train whistles on approaching
Hanover Junction to change trains

just as Abraham Lincoln did
before he spoke the Gettysburg

Address and declared the battlefield
sacred ground. Indeed, my brother

whose bones are scattered there
died for a righteous cause—to end

abusers of humans, slavery—but
to his commanding officers it was

a mere military tactic—a morality card
filled with the blood of their own
                              slaves. A derailment.

Steel wheels screech against the rails,
a plaintive cry to stop, to stop

the incivility of bigotry still prevalent
in the North. The reformation

of the heart is what's still needed.
Tell me, what kind of emancipation

happened here? What kind of joy
did the Union celebrate?

Biking the Allegheny Trail

Night train to Cumberland,
watching landscapes glide by
till we arrive with the sun,
mount our bikes and
head down to the trail.

My son, twenty yards ahead,
I twenty behind, asking him
to lead as I did with my father.

Both of us pumping hard
in and out of time,
closing the distances.

Sunlight breaking through lush greens,
wide river flowing below;
a chipmunk darts across the trail,
a robin turns these woods to song.
Bikers without names pass by
nodding to our bikes and eyes.

Tunneling darkness through to light
we pedal steadily over bridges
too high to look down, my heart
beating hard at the rescue side.

Ten miles and we rest,
sweat soaking through our shirts.
We lean our smiling bikes on trees,
take our easy breath on benches.

Climbing and coasting,
mostly steady, pedaling in sync,
we go on without thinking,
just doing what's essential.

Four days of cycling,
each a cycle of its own.
"And the wheels . . . go round and round . . ."
marrying us to the road we're on.

Then into the city traffic
walkers and bikers pass blankly.
Father and son, son and father,
we have arrived together, we have
made the trail our own.

Onslaught

My son is angry
    at the wooly adelgid,
        the emerald ash borer,
    and now the spotted lantern fly.

He is angry at people
    who let this happen
        in the name of money.

He didn't know the chestnuts
    or their blight
        written across the pages
            of our history books

telling the devastation of invasive species.

But he sees it firsthand
    in our forests—
        killing his favorite trees

as quickly as he learns their names.

Ode to the Rust Belt

There's a special place in hell
for men who sell
a perfectly good piece of land
knowing full well
it will be strip-searched,
exploited and raped
for some gravel, some oil,
hot air and sand,
some nonrenewable resource du jour.

There's a special place in hell
for men who skip town
when business is down,
leaving their debts, their tired, their poor,
all the trappings of a company town
which must burn for awhile
in hope, wild and foolish flickering
out before imploding,
a supernova underground.

There's a special place in hell
for men who see
a hundred-year-old house:
fireplace, tile, stained glass, and filigree
and plan the perfect murder,
an annihilation worthy of Christie.
Combating blight, creating space
for an asphalt lot,
a dumpster, and a Dollar Tree.

I Wait upon a Nightjar

Monk and Miles meet "'Round Midnight"
while their cool jazz breezes blow.

Shooting stars and heat lightning
now groove on infinity.

Distantly, a train yearns for her mother—
her one eye probes the dullness—
groping unfamiliar paths.

Darkness grows like summer weeds
without a single notion
from the old Chuck-will's-widow.

Rain clouds draw a grey curtain
over far lightning and stars.

Batteries die, The Blues live;
my ears, alone with the rain,
strain for sound stretched in blackness.

The train calls from the horizon,
finding rest beyond the trees.

I wait upon a nightjar
but receive only silence.
I sigh and find ways to dream.

Yinzers, n'at

"Yinz think I speak funny? Well, yinz is a jagoff!"

That sums up a drearily persistent story for those who hail from the Pittsburgh area. A story of annoying encounters with people from other parts of the country and their reactions—ranging from bemused to belittling—to the way we speak, their demeanor akin to the discomfort people exhibit when in the presence of someone speaking a foreign language.

Yet, curiously, it is also a tale of transformation from a past of embarrassment and disrepute into a source of upbeat civic pride.

Although my western Pennsylvania-born, English teacher wife strenuously disagrees, if you're from around Pittsburgh, to some degree you speak what is known as "Pittsburghese," n'at.

It is not just the instantly recognizable sonority of smeary locution—dahntahn (downtown), Jynt Iggle (Giant Eagle supermarket), meer (mirror), ornch juice (orange juice), crans (crayons), still mill (steel mill), sammich (sandwich), arn (iron, an Iron City beer), hans (hands), worsh ("Worsh your hans before dinner!"). The land has a lexicon all its own. Among the more common—nebby (nosey, gossipy), redd up (clean up), jumbo (bologna), sweeper (vacuum cleaner), gumban (rubber band), n'at (and all that; and so forth).

Although there is a difference of opinion across the country whether soft drinks are "soda" or "pop," the latter is *de rigueur* for Coke or Pepsi or Mountain Dew, n'at, in Western Pennsylvania. Order a soda and you are likely to get a sweet treat made of ice cream in flavored carbonated water topped with whipped cream and a cherry.

As with any area of the country, a region is shaped by its cultural traditions. Western Pennsylvania has been strongly influenced by the large numbers of Eastern European and Italian immigrants who were attracted to jobs in the mills during Pittsburgh's steel making heyday.

There are, of course, modern culinary delights dominating local menus—the Pittsburgh sandwich (grilled or sliced meats piled with

French fries and slaw between slabs of Italian bread), the Pittsburgh salad (salad topped with grilled meat, shredded cheese and fries), potato patch fries (French fries smothered in cheddar, bacon and any number of other toppings), and the Gobblerito (Thanksgiving dinner on a burrito).

But kielbasa, sauerkraut, potato pancakes, golumpki, kapusta and pierogi, as well as a preference for Rigatoni pasta, continue to hold a solid place in hometown hearts and taste buds. That includes wedding receptions where these foods have long been staples.

Common to wedding receptions is the cookie table—traditionally, 100 dozen hand-crafted cookies of numerous varieties in an artfully displayed buffet. The custom took hold during the Great Depression when out-of-work families could not afford expensive wedding cakes.

The pierogi is so iconic that The Pahrits (Pirates) Pierogies, racing at the end of the fifth inning at PNC Park, have taken their place as team mascots along with the Pittsburgh Parrot.

By far the emblematic signifier of the Pittsburgh area, however, is the unique and grating "yinz." The closest any other part of the country appears to come to this usage is "yous," likely some distant cousin, heard on the streets of Philadelphia and New York, n'at. The word traces to "you'uns," an inclusive plural slang used by the Scots-Irish who settled early Pittsburgh. A more inclusive "yinz all" is a common usage, as well, suggesting a seriously garbled echo of the Southern "y'all."

Not far behind is the jarring and purposely insulting "jagoff." For all its suggestion of being a fig-leaf euphemism for an indecent expression that would swiftly exclude one from polite conversation ever again, there is claim that its roots also find origin, again, with those waggish Scots-Irish. The expression is said to stem from the word "jag," meaning "thorn" or "to be pricked." Hence, the recipient of the remark being loosely—very loosely—"a thorn in one's side." In short, a jerk.

"Jag" has found its way into common parlance with hikers and parents warning their young children wandering toward a stand of thorny bushes: "Watch out for the jaggers!" The usage is so endemic that it inspired the name of the legendary Pittsburgh rock band, The Jaggerz, whose song "The Rapper" was a nationwide hit in 1970.

The linguistic influences of this argot appear to be mixed. Experts generally place the region in the great North Midland Zone that sweeps from the Mississippi River Valley, funneling up the Ohio River Valley and into the mountains of Pennsylvania, n'at. Hence, a prevailing characterization is that we speak with a "midwestern twang."

However, some experts include an intersecting Inland South Zone that follows the Appalachian Mountains from north Alabama to New York's Southern Tier. And with it, a migration from the south of that region's equally maligned and difficult to understand Appalachian dialect. I lean toward this latter idea.

One evening, my daughter—a native Central New Yorker—was watching a Frontline report on PBS that explored the abject poverty of families living in the eastern Kentucky coal fields. All the while, I was in the kitchen on the other side of our family room, back turned to the TV, busy cleaning up a sink load of dinner dishes, n'at.

About halfway through the program, my daughter complained, "They should have subtitles. I can barely understand anything these people are saying."

"Really?" I said. "I understood every word. What's wrong with you?"

No surprise, these two great linguistic flows meet in southwestern Pennsylvania. Within that confluence, some maps mark off an additional area designated as Western Pennsylvania Regional Dialect, sometimes even labeled as Pittsburgh English.

Denigration of the Pittsburgh accent has not been confined just to sneering outsiders. Well-off people living in the region dismissively viewed it as the language of an uneducated, uncouth and rowdy working class, treating it as a sign of improper upbringing, n'at.

During the 1980s, the social and economic underpinnings of the region were shaken to the core. The steel industry closed down virtually overnight and legions of the suddenly unemployed left the area in search of jobs. The exodus spread Pittsburgh speakers across the country, their numbers most noticeable during football season at NFL stadiums around the country when black-and-gold clad members of the The Steeler (Stiller) Nation show up for Stillers away games. No matter where you go, you can probably find a Stillers' bar on game day.

As with so many people who decades ago moved on to other areas of the country, irritating encounters with ill-mannered people pointing out the "funny" way I speak come with each new address. This observation is usually accompanied by the sort of amused, patronizing look that says I've just been sized up as some sort of rustic. Pretty amusing, too, how quickly their smug expressions change when I point out that they sound just as funny to me.

Naturally, Stiller Nation children have grown up embracing the mores of their home regions. For some of us ex-pats, however, that didn't count. Even though my daughter and son were born and raised in the New York's Finger Lakes region, I made sure they were steeped in the ways of what I commonly would refer to around our house as "The Old Country."

My son is fluent in Pittsburghese. He is a rock-solid fan of the Stillers, Penguins and Pahrits. On his many trips to the area, he always has a chipped-chopped ham sammich, making sure it is only Isaly's, a brand that has lived long past the regional dairy store chain of its origins. A Klondike ice cream bar is also on his menu. For my daughter's wedding in Washington, D.C,—and her international guests—she insisted the reception have a cookie table.

The reality is that Pittsburgh has long been attracting white-collar professionals from elsewhere to its first-class educational institutions, its world-class medical center and numerous Fortune 500 corporate head-quarters. But it was a fact overshadowed by the region's boisterous image of being a blue-collar, shot-and-a-beer town. That reputation faded as the factories lining the Allegheny, Monongahela and Ohio rivers disappeared from the landscape. Meanwhile the old rough-and-tumble neighbor-hoods outside the mill gates began to take on a new, upscale—some would say gentrified—character.

Today, Gen-Xers and millennials are likely to view Pittsburghese as something spoken by their grandparents and parents from the World War II and Baby Boom generations. But as the old dialect became legacy, n'at, these younger generations began to embrace it as a good-humored expression of pride of place.

On weekends and at big gatherings, people from all walks become Yinzers, n'at. On game days in particular, they are festooned in black and gold, wildly rooting for the Pens, Pahrits and Stillers. Everybody is expected to own a Turble Tahl (Terrible Towel). After the game, they flock to Primanti Bros. for Pixsburgh sammiches washed down with a couple of Arns.

For travelers to Pittsburgh (The 'Burgh) who follow the old adage, "when in Rome . . . ," it is easy to do as the Yinzers do. In addition to the usual online sources highlighting the attractions of any thriving city, one can find glossaries of Pittsburghese to enable one to banter with the citizenry. There are several more comprehensive, as well as entertaining, compilations available in print. I made sure a niece from the other side of the state had one when she enrolled at Duquesne University. One also can get a feel for the spoken word from the satirical—yet, for an old-timer like me, uncomfortably true-to-life—"Pittsburgh Dad" series on YouTube. Sort of a Yinzer edition of Babbel.

There are, of course, still those who refuse to buy into this sort of philological ribaldry. That English-teacher wife I mentioned earlier, for instance. Thankfully, her devotion to proper language—grammar, in particular—has pulled her writer husband's fat out of a rhetorical far (fire) on too many occasions to count.

That devotion, however, also triggers little ticks of disdain as I purposely slip in and out of exaggerated Yinzer-speak during normal daily conversations ("After I take my shar, I'll throw the tahls in the worsh." "The Stillers are playing the Iggles on Sunday.")

To paraphrase rockabilly legend Carl Perkins, "Yinz can take the boy out of the country, but yinz can't take the country out of the boy."

. . . n'at.

Bovinity

Bovinity. To look full on, wear shades.
A cow weighs 1600 pounds, is thinly furred,
smells of the barn that smells of her,
is wet nurse to multitudes. "The state
or quality of being a cow or ox," "dull,
stolid, slow-witted" alas elides, presumes
to measure the mind of a cow.

Divinity. To look full on, wear shades.
"Of, from, like God or a god, the state
of the divine." I'm going back to the barn.

To glean the meanings of *bovinity*
I'll take off my shoes to feel the straw,
lay my cheek on the cow's warm side,
milk her with my knowing hand, then
aim the fountain where I hear mouths.

I, Coyote

I'd near given up on these humans.
They keep their toddlers too close
for me to snatch. The man carries
bear spray when he runs in the woods
and the woman is friends with a guy
who has a night scope on his AR. That man
thinks it sport to take shots at my pack mates
and has taken down more than one.

But then the woman brought home two kittens
and kittens grow up to be cats. I love cats.
These people don't know that I dined on their last two.
The old grey tabby was easy prey. The brown mouser
put up a fight but in the end, I prevailed.
These folks are more careless
with their critters than their kids.

The woman hears our howls and thinks magic
but what she should be thinking is madness.
She's read too many stories to her kids about
my ancestors—and yes, they had special powers,
could walk on their hind legs and trick men
into going naked into the night.

The man sees my scat in the fields
and along the trails. He knows
I just can't help myself. He knows
I'll shit where I want and take
what I can get. He knows I have
more in common with his kind
than not.

David B. Prather

Onset of Autumn

All summer, cuttings make flowers bud and bloom,
severity instigating survival. But now, cicadas
fall silent, come and gone, their throaty songs
hidden in the thinnest branches. The first few

leaves have fallen. Wind goes hoarse.
It's talking more and more now
about the problems of being a nomad,
about zephyrs and breezes, and cloud breath,

about the scratchiness that goes deep
into the throat and hangs on so long
it seems nothing will ever be the same.
                              But it will.

Men take to wearing shirts again.
Women begin to cover suntanned skin.
We are deprived this beauty,
this flaunting of sexuality

under the groping hands of the sun.
The way I touch my lover, the hottest days of the year.
I miss crickets chanting me to sleep.
The sun keeps going deeper into a dark ocean,

snuffed out by lapping waves.
If I cut away my useless parts,
will I come back stronger?
I know what I can do without.

Aidan Bobik

Beyond the Grove

A gentle breeze among newly sprung leaves, green and calm—an orchestra of barely perceived instruments: little birds, recently hatched, welcoming the growing sunlight; the slow babble of the river, stained rust red from years of industry, mining, and human habitation; the faint crackling of gravel underfoot, distant but approaching. It required a certain perception and a dedicated focus on the surroundings to make out each individually. Together, however, the music they created provided an integral backdrop, barely noticed in its presence; substantially noted when gone.

On this particular day, as mid-morning turned to noon, the path was nearly abandoned, save the occasional squirrel dashing across it, or a robin flying overhead. Completed nearly three years ago, a project long in the works, it had been held up for various reasons: First was the matter of permits and permissions; an intricate web of state and local regulations and processes. Once disposed of—after two relentless years of meetings, forms, and discussions—the project languished secondly for another year and a half because of a lack of funds.

Funding was finally achieved thanks to the last will and testament of one of the few remaining town benefactors—a show of the little accumulated industrial wealth in the nearby small town. People like their benefactor had been slowly disappearing; both death and societal transformation were making their mark. Over the last year, countless volunteers, community leaders, and resources contributed to the project's construction and finalization: a walking path following a long-abandoned branch of the Buffalo and Pittsburgh Railroad.

Presently, two figures walked the path, one taller than the other. The gravel crackled and popped as they moved along, each decidedly unencumbered.

* * *

John and Maggie had so far followed the path nearly to its midpoint. Tracing what had historically been a route of growth, they glanced at the sights of its present decline: pothole-ridden backroads, fading back porches, and the slowly crumbling walls of the old mill—the centerpiece of the town. They had also, briefly, entered state game lands, clearly denoted by a signpost placed directly in view—the full spectrum of life was here, John thought.

Walking had always been a calming experience for them. Each step brought conversation—both trite and deep—the sharing of memories, hopes, and desires, and rejuvenation for the steps ahead. It was where things could be said; or, as it may be, where ideas could be abandoned after review.

John and Maggie hadn't yet ventured on this path. They preferred one closer to home but had decided on this day to give this one a try. Making their way around the bends, through wooded areas, behind residential yards, and back into the deep forest, they found it quite adequate—perhaps even more desirable than their typical place.

On a straight stretch, concern grew in John's mind.

You have to see.

The demand grew and grew, gently pushing its way to the forefront of awareness, until finally, as if being compelled, he suggested they take a detour off the prescribed path and into a slightly forested spot of oak and pine. They moved, deliberately, into the grove. Ducking under branches and over fallen trees—kin who hadn't made it—they went but a small distance until they reached an opening.

A beautiful scene greeted them. A blanket of trees, a forest of deep green filled with untold wonders. It seemed to stretch for miles. The sea of green, waves over generationally eroded mountains, was parted only by a streak of faint orange: a river of various names. Curving around multiple bends, it broke up the greenery. The lifeblood of creatures big and small—the deer, the former mill, the town. Directly in front of them, stone and rock dropped into the river below.

"Oh my God," Maggie breathed, horrified.

It was then that John noticed the deer. Lying there on the ground, calm and yet noticeably unnatural.

Crimson was seeping into the land around the animal, refueling the Earth and staining the soil. It seemed recent, and yet the deer's eyes were marbles as if already hung on someone's wall. It didn't make sense; a first incongruity. The deer's tongue poked out of an otherwise closed mouth; a visitor peering from a cave. And then there was the source of the color: rigored flesh torn from an otherwise intact body. A window into the swollen creature's body. A second incongruity.

It's all right.

The voice in the back of his mind felt distant, hollow, and yet like a comfortable embrace.

"Jesus Christ," Maggie whispered.

A putrid smell bored through the nose and into the body, into the soul. The grotesque sight imprinted into the eye, as if a ghost. And the sound, the sound crawled up the spine and nested in the ear. An incessant buzzing. The arrival of endless flies; the final nail in the coffin—the largest incongruity of them all. The tell-tale sign that death had taken.

"Is there something you're supposed to do? Do you call the Game Commission? Should we call them?" she asked.

"I don't know." It would seem, to an observer, that John couldn't keep his eyes away. He traced and retraced the diorama. His eyes followed the contours of the deer's body—or, in certain respects, where the outline would have otherwise been. *It's all right.*

It couldn't have been here very long, he thought, his own mind coming through. Yes, the smell and sound of decay had begun, but its visual counterpart had not yet arrived. Visually, it seemed so recent, still so bright, as if this had just occurred. The senses did not compute; it was still only the sight of death. And yet it felt perfectly right.

"It's so close to the path."

"I don't know," John repeated. There was something mesmerizing about it, about the way the deer held onto his thoughts, mind, and soul. How close they were to it; how it was simply there.

He didn't feel melancholic or sad. Neither, however, was there a positive aura. The place now had an unexplainable quality, the way one is drawn to an accident on the highway. Each glance away necessitated a look back. The sight juxtaposed with the smell and the sound—it couldn't compute; it did. The full spectrum of life was in front of his eyes.

Yes, it's all right.

He had, of course, seen dead deer; it was the nature of living in the area. He had even, on occasion, been their cause of death. His partner hadn't—she had never been so close to death. He sympathized with her.

"Can we just go back?"

John took it all in for one last time. The river. The trees. The sky. The rocks below. And the deer, the guardian of this place. He met its eyes—a visage between life and death.

It's all right, go.

"Okay."

* * *

Off the path, not too far from where people were intended to go, there was a spot of wildflowers—a beautiful monochromatic palette of reds.

They varied in height: some ascended to several inches; others kept low to the ground. There were shades along the full spectrum—dark burgundy to bright scarlet. Some were almost pink in pigmentation, while others approached black. They twisted and fell over each other—a controlled chaos.

Most odd, however, were the borders of the flower patch: an oval-like spot where no flowers dared to leave. The patch never grew in size, and there were never red flowers outside its bounds. It was only here—perpetually and remarkably here.

For whatever reason, the eerie flower patch seemed like a welcome mat to the vista. Some stumbled upon it—the occasional fellow aiming for moderate adventure; on one occasion young lovers who thought, "Why not?" Others were compelled to do so—either of an ingrained nature or in just this instant, a nagging that said, *see what's there, beyond the grove; you won't be disappointed.*

Incomer

I only had one condition when I moved from New York to West Virginia with my soon-to-be husband, I wanted to live in a vegetarian house. Yes, he'd said, that would be fine, though he still liked eating meat, and might want to have it from time to time, but (*Did he say this?*) don't worry, not at home. We packed my life into the bed of his pickup, drove about six hours, stopped for groceries, then turned onto a narrow road beside a small creek, tires grinding through red-brown clay.

It could've been a movie set: woods giving way to a clearing, rusted farm implements settling into the ground, a maple tree with rose-tinged golden leaves about as tall as the farmhouse, a sloping porch with a wooden swing and a wringer washer, mason jars on basement shelves holding dark floating food. I thought that love, the idea that life is an adventure, and cheap rent would make it all work. It lasted a week.

Two of his brothers showed up with a deer stretched across the roof of a station wagon, body split, organs hollowed out, tongue lolling, eyes two black stones holding less light than chunks of coal. The carcass was hoisted by a grappling hook, a steel rod pierced its hind legs, all night it hung, curling into itself, a question mark. No one spoke to me, and no one spoke about the deer, as if they had been warned to steer clear, though it did not take long to get the message. How brothers band together like an army if they sense a traitor in their midst. How one cold snap can toss pretty leaves onto the ground, show a tree for what it is. Not mine, rifles leaning against the woodbin. Not mine, the bloodstained boots on the rug. This meat saw, this grinder, the golden leaves that curl and fly, not mine.

A Field

i

Among yellow leaves and autumn's
golden light, yellow-bellied sapsuckers
seek heaven in boughs that reach
up and up. What do they know and how?

Their chisel-tipped beaks tap—
      roots and trunk
      bark and bough
      and make a perch
      I envy, wanting rest.

ii

If yellow were a field,
and it often is,
I would sneeze at goldenrod and mustard weed,
swim in deep imaginings
of sun warmed ponds,
becoming one with sunlight.

iii

When light comes bright
within me, fire beaming from
my solar plexus, Manipura
grants me balanced power
from my fire inside,
my personal sun.

iv

As autumn comes, as autumn must,
golden dust thrusts itself—
a canary or a goldfinch—
wings gliding and flapping
amidst fractured glowing light—
breath held tight.

v

Old fence posts
have lost their purpose,
tilting and leaning,
breaking and falling,
landing on gray stone.

Smoky City

[cli-cli-clack]
Dark figures in trench coats scurry across streetcar tracks, the tall buildings on the other side of the street visible only in the glow of a neon Coca-Cola sign. The caption reads, "Liberty and Fifth Avenues, 10:35 a.m."
[cli-cli-clack]
Two workmen stand beneath an ornate steel bridge and look up toward a tiny disc of sun that barely penetrates the black air. The bridge disappears into the murk just past the first pile out in the river.
[cli-cli-clack]
Cars exit the stone arches of the Liberty tubes into the translucent air. Above, the mountainside fades behind a wall of dark gray smoke.

Today, Mrs. Anundson is showing more enthusiasm than usual for social studies. Most days she's more interested in mathematics and grammar exercises, but today she's really into it as her slides clack one by one from the spinning carousel down into the bright light of the projector below. As a fourth grader, I'm still not sure I understand exactly what "social studies" is supposed to mean, and I don't think my teacher is perfectly clear on this mystery either. I know vaguely that it's supposed to be history plus other stuff. I know that the other stuff includes something called "current affairs," but beyond that it all seems a bit nebulous.

Today is a current affairs day, and we are talking about pollution. It is April, and we have just come out of the energy crisis winter of 1974. On TV, Walter Cronkite has told us about the OPEC oil embargo and showed us grainy footage of long lines of giant gas guzzlers waiting to top up at understocked filling stations.

We have also seen, a thousand times each, the Crying Indian commercial on TV. "Some people have a deep, abiding respect for the natural beauty that was once this country," the somber voiceover admonishes us time and again, "and some people don't." As the stoic brave weeps amidst urban decay, we are reminded again and again that "People start pollution. People can stop it."

[cli-cli-clack]
Two Gotham-style skyscrapers reach toward the smoky sky. Their façades are blurred by clouds of smoke, their pyramidal tops disappearing into the black clouds above.
[cli-cli-clack]
Wet cars shine as they follow streetcar lines into the darkened canyon of tall, ornamented office buildings. The caption tells us it's "midday," but the streetlights are on, and the neon of street-level shops is visible only for the next quarter block.
[cli-cli-clack]
A church's Gothic spire shoots up through the darkened sky. It must be daytime because the sun glows dully through the heavy smoke.

Today's lesson is a follow-up from our social studies lesson last month on the history of the Robber Barons, those admirably greedy capitalists of the Gilded Age. Pittsburgh had loomed large in that unit, too, especially the steel industry giants: Andrew Carnegie, Henry Clay Frick, and J.P. Morgan.

I remember a two-page spread in our Holt, Rinehart, and Winston social studies textbook: tiny workers manning a giant vat of molten iron, in a massive mill that looked a lot like hell. On the next page, Carnegie's block-long mansion in New York and his even larger museums and library in Pittsburgh.

Now Mrs. Anundson is explaining to us that Pittsburgh's smoky skies and smelly rivers are the direct result of the very industry that has made it so powerful and mighty. The city is dirty and dangerous so the rest of the world can have steel. She tells us about smokestacks that choked the entire city with thick black soot, mountainsides that were ripped open to extract coal, and toxic wastes flowing directly from those factories and mines into all three of the city's rivers (but especially the Monongahela).

Pittsburgh's air, she says, was so dirty that sometimes the city had to turn on streetlights during daylight hours. Businessmen had to keep a change of clothes in their office, in case the walk to a restaurant for lunch left their starched white shirts gray. It was so bad that if you blew your irritated nose onto a clean white handkerchief, your snot would be black with toxic dust. My classmates are suitably impressed by the nastiness of it all, and several of them state that they sure are glad we live in the country, where the air is clean and there are lots of trees. They can't imagine why anyone would want to live in such a hellish place, which they know is not just dirty, but also dangerous.

[cli-cli-clack]
In the foreground an ornate clock marks 12:10 pm., but the streetscape beyond fades into a foggy darkness. The streetlights are lit all the way down the street, but all that's visible even half a block away are the neon signs of shops and theaters: Harris, Loftis, King's, Palace.
[cli-cli-clack]
Two girls in trim dresses stand stiffly side by side in front of a curvy early-forties Chevrolet sedan. Behind them, uneven glimpses of a city skyline poke through the heavy dark smoke.
[cli-cli-clack]
The same two girls stand alone in front of the elaborate ironwork of a bridge railing. Down on the river below, debris floats among clouds of daytime gray.

Mrs. Anundson is going off-script. She has transitioned from the slides provided as a supplement to our textbook to photos from her own family album. There she is, a teen in a modest A-line dress, witnessing with her own two eyes the filthy air and contaminated water of downtown Pittsburgh.

Suddenly I understand why she is so enthusiastic about this lesson on pollution. Unlike all the history we've been studying, unlike even the other current affairs of the time—Watergate and the OPEC crisis—now we are talking about something that she herself has witnessed, that she can describe from memory in all of its vibrant colorless intensity.

Now my classmates are joining in for one of the liveliest conversations we've ever had in our usually dreary social studies class. Bobby Brinkley reminds us for the eighty-seventh time that he had been chosen to attend the nearby cutting ceremony for the U.S. capitol Christmas tree that past November (randomly, the principal assured us). "Yeah," he continues, "cities like D.C. must be so crummy that they have to come all the way to the Allegheny National Forest to get a damn—I mean danged—Christmas tree." The other kids nod in agreement as Mrs. A. rewards Bobby with a rare smile for having policed his own swearing this time.

I have to say I'm a little disoriented by this lesson. The thing is, my family and I moved to this small Pennsylvania town just eight months ago—from Pittsburgh! Though we now live three hours farther north, on the edge of the national forest in my parents' hometown of Kane, Pittsburgh is where I was born and where I spent the first eight years of my life. This inferno of air so dirty you can taste it and rivers flowing with fluorescent slime doesn't seem anything like the Pittsburgh I know. Yeah, Pittsburgh has steel mills, but it also has lots of trees.

Yeah, you wouldn't want to go swimming in the Monongahela, but it's not going to catch on fire like the Cuyahoga in downtown Cleveland. To me, Pittsburgh is nothing like the filthy city in the dreary slides. For me, Pittsburgh is my very own paradise lost: Though our mail was addressed to "Pittsburgh, PA 15205," we didn't actually live in the city of Pittsburgh. For my family, home was the quiet suburban borough of Thornburg, where oversized Arts and Crafts bungalows dot a wooded hillside five miles out from downtown. Our own house was a rambling Craftsman of heavy stone walls and Tudor beams just down the hill from the low-slung Spanish Revival school and the large community park where I met up each summer day with my neighborhood friends.

Though we didn't technically live in the city of Pittsburgh, we did spend a lot of time there. My mom would pile my brothers and me into the red Mercury Marquis, and then we'd wind up the hill out of Thornburg. We'd pass the terraced Dutch colonial townhouses of Pennsbury Village and then weave through the leafy borough of Rosslyn Farms until we reached the Parkway West. The parkway passed a few factories and gritty working-class neighborhoods on the way downtown but mostly wound through wooded mountains. When we reached the Fort Pitt Tunnel, we'd enter the tube into what looked like any old wooded Pennsylvania mountainside. In the tunnel, with its narrow lanes and dirty white-tile walls, we kids would hold our breath. Then we'd exhale, squealing with delight, to the light on the other side of the mountain, the whole city laid out in front of us.

Coming out of the Fort Pitt Tunnel onto the Fort Pitt Bridge, the first thing that caught our eyes was the skyline of towering office buildings. The undisputed king was the sixty-four-story U.S. Steel Building, a rust-colored monument to the city's defining industry. There were the steps of the pyramid atop the bright-white Gulf Oil building and the glimmering stainless-steel panels of the Gateway Center complex, where my Dad worked. And right in the front row of buildings were the golden-framed windows of the Pittsburgh Hilton, where my parents had spent their short honeymoon ten years earlier.

If you looked to the left from the bridge, you would see the famed golden triangle, where the city narrows so the Allegheny and the Monongahela Rivers can unite to form the mighty Ohio. A giant fountain was being constructed at the point itself, connected to the skyline by a new green park in which lay the ruins of the original Fort Pitt, a park that would fill with art each summer for the Three Rivers Arts Festival.

On the rivers themselves, long flat barges and an old-fashioned steamboat called the *Good Ship Lollipop* floated beneath the rows of yellow steel bridges. Each bridge was a little bit different from the others, except for the famed "Three Sisters" bridges, nearly identical as they crossed the Allegheny at Sixth, Seventh, and Ninth Streets.

Straight across from the point, on the far side of downtown, sat the giant Three Rivers Stadium, where we would go to Pirates games on sticky summer nights and once to a Steeler game on a bitter cold winter afternoon. And if we looked behind us as we descended from the bridge into downtown, we could see back across the Monongahela to the steep wooded mountains on our side of the river, where the bright red Duquesne Incline made its way up and down the nearly vertical hillside below Mount Washington.

Downtown (or dahntahn, as more vernacular Pittsburghers would call it) was full of men like my dad in sharp gray business suits, but it was also the home of Kaufmann's, Horne's, and Gimbel's, old-school big-city department stores. I remember the cold light of a snowless December afternoon, my mom pulling me by the hand, walking too fast for me to keep up, as we went from one store to the next. Kaufmann's, in particular, was magic to my child's eyes, the smell of perfume samples and crisp new clothes, the sparkle of expensive Christmas decorations, the promised treat of hot chocolate and a giant cookie in the Tic Toc restaurant.

Downtown was magic, but Mom often took us kids past downtown, either winding along the Monongahela or cutting through the down-and-out Hill District. Either way, we would end up in Oakland, where the University of Pittsburgh's Cathedral of Learning—a quirky forty-two-story skyscraper in the Gothic style—was the crown jewel in a neighborhood of broad leafy boulevards and one monumental building after another.

Our two favorite locations in Oakland were both part of the giant complex of Carnegie museums, high-drama buildings in late nineteenth-century classical styles that had been blackened by years of exposure to the industry that made Andrew Carnegie so rich in the first place. For my little brothers, as for most other kids I knew, the hands-down favorite was the Carnegie Museum of Natural Science, one of the best dinosaur museums in the world. We would pass impatiently by dusty dioramas of daily life among the world's primitive peoples to arrive at the piéce de resistance: the gigantic skeleton of a real Tyrannosaurus Rex, perched menacingly on his enormous hind legs, an almost audible growl evident in his mouth full of sharp teeth that seemed as tall as us.

The dinosaurs were cool, but for me the best part of a trip to Oakland was a visit to the Carnegie Free Library, just around the corner from the dinosaur museum. The children's section of the library was huge, packed with more colorful books than any one person could possibly read over all the long years of childhood. I would explore the books or sit to listen as a sweet old lady librarian chanted the story hour. We came to Oakland frequently enough that I could always check out a couple of books, knowing that we would bring them back before their due dates two weeks later. The Carnegie was the site of the first dates in my life-long love affair with reading.

The bell has rung in Mrs. Anundson's classroom, so now we take a short bathroom break before transitioning from social studies to math. But the social studies lesson sticks with me as my family and I continue settling into our new life in Kane.

As I pay closer attention to what the kids and adults around me say, I learn that most Kane residents view cities much differently than I do. To me, cities are magical places with glittering office towers, candy-themed steamboats, delightfully scary dinosaurs, and more books than you could ever read. But all these kids can see in the green, hilly city of my birth is dirty air and crime and overcrowding. To them the city is dangerous, as bad for your health as it is for your moral well being. We are lucky to live in the safe embrace of the Allegheny National Forest, and why would you possibly want to leave?

Even my dad, who used to be one of those suited businessmen in downtown Pittsburgh, joins in. On top of endlessly extolling the wonders of the great outdoors here up north, Dad loves to recite to his friends in Pittsburgh and other cities the local police report, identical every single day in the Kane Republican newspaper and on radio station WKZA: "The police report that they have nothing to report." Like other Kane residents, he shudders at news reports of muggings, murders, and auto thefts in places like New York City and brags of leaving our house unlocked when we go on vacation, the keys in the ignition while we sleep at night.

Me, though, I'm a skeptic. I was always happy in our bucolic suburb and on our adventures in the big city. We had plenty of woods to play in, but somehow, they weren't quite as muddy as the cold woods here in Kane. It seemed more civilized to me to be able to step from the woods onto a sidewalk or paved road.

I also felt plenty safe back in Thornburg, where we kids could play unsupervised in the borough park just up the hill. In fact, I felt a lot safer in Thornburg than I do here in this small town where everybody seems to be exactly like everybody else. A sensitive boy, a little effeminate, I can't seem to crack the rigid local code of acceptable masculine behavior, and it is exhausting trying. I don't feel safe when the other kids call me a sissy and sometimes worse.

The truth is that Pittsburgh has cleaned up its act since Mrs. Anundson went there back when she was a young Miss Lindquist in the 1940s. The domestic steel industry had begun its tumultuous decline, and strict new pollution laws regulated those mills that were still producing, which led to significantly cleaner air and water. Most houses had switched from coal heat to natural gas, and the skies had cleared.

Things are not perfect by any means. You can't clean up 150 years' worth of toxic industrial waste in just twenty years. The Technicolor efflu-ence that Miss Lindquist witnessed on the surface of the Monongahela has long since passed down the Ohio and then the Mississippi to mess up the Gulf of Mexico. But no doubt the silt on the bottom of the river remains toxic—and will remain toxic for many years to come.

The energy crisis spring of 1974 transitions into a gentle northern Pennsylvania summer. Still feeling defensive in the face of the locals' dis-dain for my urban birthplace—and for cities in general—I start observ-ing more closely the wooded mountains that surround my new home in Kane. As I walk rutted trails that clearly used to be roads, I can't help but notice the stone and metal ruins that seem to lurk everywhere beneath the fern-carpeted understory, evidence of some sort of mysterious earlier civilization.

An amateur archaeologist, I learn to identify industrial and domestic ruins in my wanderings through the woods: Half-buried railroad tracks lead to a large tin shed where a perfectly preserved steam engine is parked for posterity. A rainbow glint in the mossy concrete under our feet might signal a half-buried glass brick or electrical insulator. Rusty metal can appear anywhere: ten-foot-diameter tanks, pipes to nowhere, antique oil wells that are still pumping away.

The largest and most noticeable ruin is the red clapboard structure leaning perilously onto the railroad tracks a hundred yards farther down the unnamed dirt road from our house. Peering through the dirty windows of this crooked depot, I identify a huge, decommissioned meat cooler and an old-style general store with a bank of postal boxes labeled U.S. Mail. More mysterious is the wood-paneled office with the sign "Otto Chemical Company" hanging outside. How, I wonder, does one make chemicals in the middle of the woods, and why is there no factory visible anywhere?

The domestic remains feature stone steps to nowhere, or perhaps to a crumbling, half-buried stone foundation. They tend to be lined up in rows, just like the rows of still-extant factory houses scattered here and there all around us. Clues to a domestic past can also be found in signs of flora inappropriate to the overgrown forest: a wormy apple tree here, a German Iris there, a patch of foxglove or brilliant blue lupines never seen in wilder parts of the area.

The industrial remains are more impressive. In one clearing the size of a soccer field sit the ruins of an old glass factory. There, the flatness of the site masks hidden dangers: down by the railroad tracks there's a six-foot drop-off, probably a former loading dock for getting the finished glass products onto the train. About twenty feet in from that, there's a hole about fifteen feet square and five feet deep; the bottom of this depression is strewn with random debris, so it's hard to tell whether there's solid ground below. Then, toward the other end zone of the soccer field stand the hulking metal skeletons of giant ovens, their rusty doors hanging open on crooked hinges. For me there's something satisfying in the glasswork ruins' imposition of architectural angles on a natural site. Or maybe it's the imposition of the riotous nature that has overrun the architectural angles. The biggest pleasure of the glassworks site, though, is the hunt for treasures. I unearth a half-buried glass brick here and an electrical insulator there, prizes I can take to add to my collection at home.

My personal favorite ruin is a magical stone pool on the hillside above the glassworks, whose solid walls dam a cold stream from higher up the hill. I climb the uneven concrete steps, pass through the unlocked chain link gate, and come upon clear, cold water in which darts the brown brilliance of a school of brook trout. Dad doesn't let us kids fish in this pool, though. He tells us it wouldn't be a fair battle with the fish, who are trapped here and have not learned how to protect themselves from various types of predators, unlike the wilder trout in the streams. I wonder if this is the real reason he doesn't let us fish here, or if maybe it's because the fish themselves might be carrying some kind of toxic postindustrial residue.

Years later, I'll learn that what I know as the Allegheny National Forest was once called the "Allegheny brush heap." By the time the Forest Service came in and bought up half the area's land on the cheap in 1923, the timber, tanning, and chemical industries had basically clear-cut the entire Allegheny plateau region. There really was no forest to speak of, just a wasteland of stumps and scrub and hardly any deer. The forest we know now—both the Allegheny National Forest and the privately owned mountainsides around it—had all grown up out of that brush heap over many years. The profitable hardwoods like black cherry and red maple that the timber industry so prizes have only been able to thrive due to the open sunlight of the widespread clear-cuts, creating a new, carefully cultivated generation of trees that bears little resemblance to the aboriginal forest of hemlock, pine, and beech.

So, it turns out that our rural area has its own dirty past. Maybe the factories were smaller than the ones in Pittsburgh, but they left the forests decimated and the soil and water contaminated. Maybe these plants shut down earlier—in most cases, before my parents were even born—but this is hardly some undefiled wilderness.

I'll give it to my fellow Kane residents that their post-industrial woods are even prettier than Pittsburgh's, less disturbed as they are by active industry. I'll also let them feel safe in this place where everybody appears to be just like everybody else, but when I get my chance, I'll be out of here. I'll take my unmanly self and go out into the dangerous world and live in the biggest cities I can find: Cairo, Los Angeles, New York, Mexico, São Paulo. I'll come back on vacations to see my family, and I'll appreciate the fresh brisk air and the trees all around. Then, when the week is up, my mom will drive me three hours south to the Pittsburgh airport, and I'll fly off to live my life in the big, bad city.

Radio Preacher

The Radio Preacher has had it
with heathens, unbelievers, and idolaters
who worship affluence and worldliness.

He is done with prosperity sermonizers
who claim that believers may
obtain riches from God,
simply by writing out a check.

*I don't care if you've been dunked in
every creek in the county, so
the minners know you by name,
unless you're saved and washed in the blood
you are lost forever.*

*I've had it with unclean spirts and
educated fools who obey Satan:
movie stars, athletes, celebrities, college professors.
Most are in hell or heading there soon.*

College professors?
A little close to home.

He has more:
*Sometimes I'm asked to write a letter
of reference for college and I'll say
what good Christians these students are.*

I always close with:
I hope this child doesn't get some
God-hating, infidel professor, who will
drag'em down to hell with'em.

Here it comes.
Surely, this time
Radio Preacher will call out my name
right through the airwaves.
But he fades off
like a forecasted storm
that never comes.

Jewing Him Down

At the Victory Elementary School meeting outside of Clintonville, PA; Natalie, the go-to gal for anything volunteer related, was describing her conversation with the grocery store owner. We're trying to raise more money for a new playground, and she's been hard at work organizing fundraisers. They're talking raffle: $5.00 a ticket, winner take all—in this case, huge pounds of meat, plus a freezer to store it in. And meat's no joke in southern Venango county, rural, poorest region in the state. We're meeting in the art room of the elementary school—crouching on child-sized chairs pulled up against the low table, Natalie and Tammy's kids drawing on the chalkboard. "So I was talking to the guy," Natalie wants to get the best price she can—"you know, trying to chew him down . . ."

And suddenly the room froze, and though her lips kept moving, it felt like all the words that followed were like the way wheels keep spinning when the car has already spilled over the side of the hill.

I like Natalie. The school would fall apart without her. And the kids need a new playground. The wheels slowed down to a standstill.

Sasquatch

A story on NPR yesterday
about Bigfoot being 60 years old
made me think of my late husband Kevin's sighting
in 1978 by the DaShuttes River
in Bend, Oregon,
and how the first sighting was
in the year 1957, when I was 2.

He claimed it was an upright ape,
lumbering across the river from him
A *Gigantopithecus*—the correct Latin term.
He said he was absolutely sure—
the Thai stick he smoked had nothing to do with it.
He would have snapped a picture
if he'd had a cell phone, but it was in late 1978.

Is it a wonder that sightings are made in the backwoods
and forests of West Virginia,
and that they believe in its existence
in the Appalachian Mountain communities?
Could there be a primate species
we have not captured and studied?
Could this mythology continue to entrap
and intoxicate us with make-believe and
throw us back to medieval thought?
Is it not unlike the study of ESP,
alien migration or paranormal activity—
where we are sure or not sure?
Confident or not confident?
Like a belief
that there is a white male God in heaven?

Punxsutawney

Inspired by a photograph by B.A. Van Sise from the Elsewhere series

As before, the 757 flies below the clouds
and not much above the trees, the airport
just over the ridge, but even the cows
look at each other as if something isn't
right, as if an alien is invading the sanctity
of their farm. The chickens already fleeing
to the coop, the barnyard dog is nowhere
in sight. I flashback to a heavy jet caught
in Texas rain with severe wind shear on final
approach into Dallas-Fort Worth back in '85,
and to that Dustin Hoffman film *Hero* where
he enters a burning plane after it went down
in a thunderstorm, to steal wallets. Instead
he saves a bunch of passengers from the fire.

But in this picture, there's no storm, no failing
engine—no billowing smoke I can see, yet
the plane is in a dive. All I know of what to do
is pray. Hope it's my imagination or an optical
illusion. Reason that the cows' unsettledness
is due to a low-pressure system moving in
as it so often does on cool September mornings
over Pennsylvania farms. Maybe it's just another
Groundhog Day . . . and the plane keeps flying.

Love in a Small World

"Sounds to me like one of them love at first sight things," said Radaker.

Huffman couldn't argue. Maybe his friend was right. He'd just seen the girl for the first time, and she wouldn't get out of his head. She'd come into Siebert's Women's Clothing, where Huffman worked, where he knew most of the customers, Hartsgrove being the small town that it is. But this one he'd never seen before. He thought maybe Radaker might know who she was, so he'd described her: slender but shapely where it mattered in his estimation, her black hair straight back in a no-nonsense cut. Long eyelashes she looked out from under when he gave her her change, dark eyes that grabbed him by the scruff of the neck and shook.

They were sitting at the counter in the Country Club, four doors up from Siebert's, the little restaurant on Main Street where they often met for lunch.

Huffman said, "Wouldn't that be impossible?"

"Wouldn't what be?"

"Love at first sight. I always heard love was blind."

Radaker said, "Good one," sipping his root beer float through a straw being strangled by his carpenter's hands. It always astonished Huffman how, even sprinkled with sawdust, the wave of carefully combed hair that crowned his friend's forehead remained perpetually unperturbed, as though varnished in place.

"You gonna eat the rest of that?" Radaker said, nodding toward the remnants of Huffman's tuna salad sandwich sitting neglected on the plate. His own hoagie was history.

"No—you want it?"

Radaker was already reaching. "So what are you going to do about it?"

"About what?" said Huffman. "About the girl?" Would she ever come back into the store? Would he ever see her again? "Not too sure what I can do."

"You can find out who she is for starters," Radaker said around a mouthful of tuna. "Somebody's gotta know who she is."

"I suppose." Huffman was elsewhere, a memory drifting into his mind of a man who climbed up the iron girders of the old bridge arching high over Sandy Lick Creek at the bottom of Pershing Street. Someone in the crowd looking up said the man was love sick. His girlfriend had dumped him, someone else said. The man was in uniform. It must have been during the war, years ago, when he was a kid. Huffman didn't care much for childhood memories. Childhood memories always brought him back to the murder, to the fear and dread, to his cousin's execution—memories he'd be pleased to forget.

He remembered seeing the wind high overhead catch the man's tie and fling it straight out from his neck, as though an invisible hand had grabbed it, the wind trying to yank him off the bridge, dash him onto the rocks of the creek below.

Love at first sight. A dangerous thing.

* * *

"No," Elva said. "I'm afraid I couldn't tell you. I haven't been in there in years." Gracie had been describing the young man, the sales clerk, she'd encountered earlier that day, wondering who he might be.

"You don't shop at Siebert's?" Gracie said.

"No," said Elva, tapping her cigarette on the edge of the ashtray. They were standing at the nurse's station. Elva, a short lady, a head shorter than Gracie, moved the ashtray closer, tilting her head back, exhaling a dainty stream of smoke. "And I don't think you should, either. Bruce Siebert is on the hospital board—he doesn't support the nurses, so I don't support his store. Wein's has just as good a selection, and better prices, too." When Gracie didn't respond, when she only frowned at the ashtray, Elva added, "Of course Wein's doesn't have a good-looking salesman."

"That right there's the problem," Gracie said.

"What's he look like?"

"Reddish hair, nice build. Kind of a baby face," Gracie said. "He looks a little bit like Alan Ladd."

"Sounds to me like you're smitten."

"Once smitten, twice shy," Gracie said. *Smitten*. Leave it to Elva, her friend—her only friend, really, in this little town that was new to her—to come up with a word such as that. Elva was older; perhaps it was a word from the previous generation. Smitten. *Was* she smitten? Or just lonely? She was that, of course, but as she thought about the face of the young man, the puppy warm eyes, she thought it was the first time since she'd moved to Hartsgrove—the first time ever?—that she'd encountered another person across an open divide, with no apparent barriers between them. She wanted to know his name. She wanted to know much more than his name. But how many pairs of hose, or garters, or gloves could she possibly buy?

Mrs. Carrier came through the double doors down the corridor in her haughty amble, nurse's cap nested snugly in its curly gray nest, like a crisp, white dove. At the nurse's station, she looked down her nose at Gracie and Elva, an eyebrow arched. "Mrs. Morley's vitals are to be taken every thirty minutes," she said.

"Gracie was on her way," said Elva. "She was just telling me about a young man who works down at Siebert's. We were wondering how she could meet him."

Mrs. Carrier's face darkened. "Wonder on your own time," she said. "You have a ward full of patients who are not terribly concerned about Miss Wolfgang's love life."

The two older women locked hostile gazes for a second or two under Gracie's watchful eye, breaking away just short of challenge. As Mrs. Carrier made her way around the counter, Elva stubbed out her cigarette rudely.

Gracie thought she heard Evla mutter, "Old Biddy," loudly enough that Mrs. Carrier must have heard it as well.

If she did, she let it pass. Gracie, to whom such contention might normally be troubling, found herself distracted instead by Mrs. Carrier's words: *Miss Wolfgang's love life*. Such a hollow phrase, of course, intended no doubt to be ironic: Gracie had no love life, as Mrs. Carrier was surely aware.

A light came on above 317: Mr. Stockdale, in need of her bedpan again. As Gracie hurried to duty, the image of the young man looking at her from across the store, a look of anticipation fulfilled, as though he'd been waiting for her all along, faded away—she had no love life after all, only hope—and the face of her Aunt Lucy took its place. Gracie didn't remember her aunt well, but she remembered her with affection. Aunt Lucy had barged into her mind often in the short time since she'd moved to Hartsgrove, for Gracie had, in a sense, followed in her aunt's footsteps, moving to the bigger town from tiny Sugargrove to find work. But it was here, in Hartsgrove, that Aunt Lucy's life had been cut short.

Gracie was only six when her aunt had been murdered in the railyard signal tower where she worked by a night watchman from the glass plant nearby. The words—*Miss Wolfgang's love life*—lent the memory a new poignancy; had her aunt ever even had a love life?

She remembered Aunt Lucy rubbing daisies under her chin to determine whether or not she liked butter. She did. And she remembered Aunt Lucy tickling her knee to determine whether or not she liked the boys, and Gracie had tried not to laugh, tried to hold back, but in the end, she was helpless. She finally surrendered, giggling and laughing, reluctantly, against her will, against her better judgment liking the boys.

* * *

"Gracie Wolfgang," Huffman said. "As soon as she came in again, I just came right out and asked her."

"No sense beating around the mulberry bush," Radaker said.

"Yeah. Especially so early in the morning."

Radaker frowned at what he took to be a non-sequitur, looking at his watch. It was not morning. "That name don't sound familiar," he said, hunched over, gripping the wheel, peering intently through the windshield of his old pickup. Even on a beautiful afternoon, he drove as though he were tacking into a heavy storm. "She ain't from around here?"

"No," Huffman said, "she isn't. She's from Sugargrove. Just moved down here a couple months ago."

At the bottom of Valley Street, Radaker turned onto Mill Street just before the bridge, then into the rutted entryway of Bowersox Lumber

Yard. Huffman grimaced as though at a bad smell. "Thought you were going to Mason's," he said.

"Smokey's is cheaper," said Radaker. "A penny saved is worth two in the bush."

"I suppose. Me, I prefer to do business with *homo sapiens*, though. Neanderthals can be a little tough to deal with sometimes."

Radaker shrugged. "Neanderthals need love too."

"If you say so," said Huffman.

Maneuvering around the rusted hulk of a forklift, Radaker backed up to a shelter where boards lay heaped in untidy piles. He climbed out and began examining two-by-fours, eyeballing down the edges for warp, while Huffman, opening his door with a loud, rusty squawk, stepped out and took in the squalor. From around the corner of a long, semi-dilapidated barn—unlike Mason's, there was no office, no showroom—Smokey Bowersox appeared. Squalor itself. For as long as Huffman could remember, Bowersox had been a fixture in the town, big and ugly, loud and mean, his slab of a face sheathed in uneven stubble, his hair as greasy and tangled as a mountain man's. Huffman could only speculate what might be living in there. "Radaker, you son of a bitch," Bowersox hollered, "you stealing my boards again?"

Bowersox always hollered. Even after he was standing beside them, he hollered. "Who you got with you? Why, if it ain't Huffman! Henry Huffman—how come you ain't up selling bras and panties?"

"Why? You need some new ones, Smokey?"

Radaker guffawed. A dark cloud passed over Bowersox's face. He said, "How's your old man, old Killer George?"

Killer George. The nickname Bowersox had bestowed on Huffman's father, a nickname harkening back to the nasty business with Huffman's cousin years ago: His cousin, Oscar, had gone to the chair for killing a woman in the railyard signal tower when Huffman was only a boy. But had he been guilty? Huffman always had his doubts, as did others, but many of those others blamed Huffman's father, George, Oscar's uncle, instead. Bowersox, though, so far as Huffman knew, was the only one who called his father Killer George, at least to his face.

"He's keeping his diaper clean, Smokey—how 'bout you?"

"Shit, Huffman—I shit bigger turds than you do every day."

Huffman and Radaker rolled their eyes in unison. Radaker said, "Smokey, it's 'I shit bigger turds than *you* every day,' not 'bigger turds than you *do*.' That don't make no sense."

Bowersox only glowered. He had no time for the finer points of insults.

As they pulled away with a bedful of boards, Bowersox hollered, "Say howdy to Killer George for me!"

Radaker muttered, "No sense being ugly if you ain't dumb too."

Huffman's mind was elsewhere. The sunlight glittering on the water of the Red Bank Creek brought Gracie to his mind, again—not that she'd been far from it the whole day. The glitter of the sun like the glitter in her eyes, in her smile, both bold and shy at once. How she'd smiled in the store—her mouth in a shy little o, almost the shape of a heart—when he'd asked her her name, and the charge, an almost electric buzz, when he'd touched her hand, giving her her change. And how his feet had seemed to lift off the floor when she said yes—yes, she'd love to go see a movie with him. *Creature from the Black Lagoon* was starting Friday at The Columbia.

Love at first sight? The cliché must exist for a reason.

How to account for the newness, the freshness of this feeling? Why, in all his years, had he never experienced a feeling like this? She was *not from around here*—that was why. Not from around here.

She'd never heard of his cousin Oscar, never heard of Killer George, of his mother running off, of the murder and scandal that had laid waste to the Huffman family nearly twenty years ago. When Gracie looked at him she couldn't see the invisible sign around his neck, the sign that said, *Look at me! Look at what my cousin did! Look at what my mother did!*—the invisible sign that everyone else saw, had always seen.

Radaker dropped him off at his car behind Siebert's. "Feel like a beer?"

"I better get on home. Clean up after Killer George."

"Listen," said Radaker with a tap on the wheel. "Don't pay him any mind. Consider the source. You ought to just let it roll off you like water off a duck's ears."

"Oh, I do. Hell, I shit bigger turds than Bowersox does every day."

Radaker laughed. Huffman paused, putting his hand to the back of his head—a habit, as if trying to coax out the thought—he said, "Let me ask you something, Earl—a few years ago, it was during the war I think, or just after it, some fella climbed up on the bridge at the bottom of Pershing—do you remember that?" Radaker dipped his eyebrow, scratched his chin.

"He climbed the whole way up on top," Huffman said, "everybody thought he was going to jump, this big crowd down below, somebody said his girlfriend had dumped him. I don't remember who it was—don't know if I ever knew. Anyhow, I can't remember what happened, how it ended. Do you know what I'm talking about?"

"Can't say as I do," Radaker said. "Don't ring a bell at all."

* * *

When Huffman got home he smelled something burnt—not for the first time. He took the pot off the stovetop: something in it was charred beyond recognition. In the living room he found his father in his wheelchair in front of the television, his head tilted to one side staring at the picture, little more than a haze of blurry lines. He walked over to the television. His father didn't look up. It sounded like Arthur Murray. Not until Huffman adjusted the rabbit ears and the picture came in clearly did his father finally look up. Killer George was in a bad way.

"That's all you have to do, Pop."

"Oh," his father said, as if remembering, "yeah."

He looked at his son's face, bafflement clawing toward clarity.

"Henry," he added.

He'd grown blubbery since he'd been consigned to his wheelchair, and his hair, always long and greasy, was even longer and greasier now, and grayer, as if from mildew. He no longer attempted to tuck it behind his ears, as he'd always done before, his last pretense of grooming. Although Killer George could fend for himself, more or less, bordering on less, he was addled.

He was in a wheelchair because he was addled—having stepped off the ladder when he was changing a lightbulb, having forgotten he was on a ladder, cracking his spine in the process—and he was addled because his wife, Elsie, Huffman's mother, had bashed him on the head with a cast-iron skillet. And that had been only the aftermath of the mayhem.

The burnt smell faded away, overcome by the rancid smell of shit—what he'd told Smokey about George keeping his diaper clean wasn't entirely true. "Pop," Huffman said, "you want me to help you get cleaned up?"

His father didn't answer. The rabbit ears drooped, the picture went hazy, and Killer George's head wilted to one side along with it.

The sins of the father, mused Huffman.

* * *

"Henry Huffman," Gracie said. "He just came right out and introduced himself."

"So now you know—good," said Elva, but her attention was elsewhere. Except for a glance, her eyes never left the batter. They were sitting in the bleachers behind home plate, Elva's husband, Jacey, on the mound for the Hartsgrove Grays, and her son, Jimmy, roaming, under the bleachers, behind the dugouts, down along the fence by the first base line, out to the scoreboard in the tall grass beyond the fence. Lofty old maples and elms lined the creek, throwing late afternoon shadows across the outfield.

Jacey retired the Harmony Mills Miners one-two-three in the top of the first. When the last man had grounded weakly to third, Elva turned to Gracie. "So? He introduced himself, and? Anything else?"

"And he asked me out," said Gracie, releasing her pent-up smile.

"Well, good for you," Elva said. "I'm so glad you're finally meeting someone, finally getting out—I remember how lonely I was when I first moved here, and I had Jacey and Jimmy. Where are you going?"

"To the movies, I think. *Creature from the Black Lagoon* is showing, he said."

"Oh, I heard that's supposed to be scary."

"Scary doesn't bother me," Gracie said. "At least not in the movies."

When the lead-off batter for the Grays stepped to the plate, Elva's attention again switched allegiance. "Come on, Billy!" she yelled. "Get a hit!"

Gracie closed her eyes. Warm afternoon sunlight on her face, surrounded by happy people urging Billy to get a hold of one, Gracie conjured up the face of the young man, Henry Huffman. Sure enough, just as it had in her room, just as it had as she was walking down the hill to the ballpark to meet Elva, her breath turned shallow, goosebumps swept over her arms and up her spine, and the tiny hairs on the back of her neck stood up and cheered. All at the thought of a face. At the sound in her mind of his voice. Surely it had happened before, Gracie thought, but if it had, she could not remember when: that the thought of another person could cause actual, physical sensations in her body. A heat, a physical urgency, passed through her, dancing lightly in her stomach.

She'd been apprehensive—frightened?—about moving to Hartsgrove in the first place, the same place where her aunt had met her end. She remembered the damage the killing had done, her mother's face twisted and tearful, unrecognizable, as they stood over the hole in the ground by the trees, where the long wooden box that they said held her aunt had been lowered into the ground. She remembered refusing to give up the rose, the pretty rose her mother had given her, when they told her to throw it into the hole on top of the box. They'd finally had to take it away from her, and she'd screamed, throwing a tantrum instead of the rose. She remembered the picture in the newspaper of a big, mean man in bib overalls, the man they said killed her Aunt Lucy, the man they said went to the electric chair. For a long time—maybe still—the big, mean man in the newspaper looked like every man she saw, especially every man she saw when she went away to nurses' training in Erie, every man away from tiny Sugargrove.

But Gracie refused to give in. When old Dr. Fetterman retired, and she heard Hartsgrove Hospital was hiring, she left Sugargrove to move to the place where her aunt had been murdered. It was this same determination that led her to return to Siebert's on the flimsiest of pretenses—*another* woolen scarf?—to reach out to this man, this new sort of man, this man with a gentle face, a gentle touch. Now, the sounds of people living life all around her, the heat of the sun on her face, she thought of that gentle man, and she soaked up the sounds of celebration.

"What did you say his name was again?"

Gracie opened her eyes. Elva was looking at her, though the inning wasn't over. "Henry Huffman," Gracie said.

"Oh, yes," Elva said. "Right."

When Elva said nothing else, when she turned away to watch the batter take a called third strike, Gracie said, "Why?"

Elva looked again at her friend. "Why what?"

"Do you know him?"

"Henry Huffman? No. Not really. I've heard of him is all," Elva said. But that was not what the look on her face said. The troubled knot on her brow said that was not all.

* * *

Gracie made the first move. Once or twice Henry had reared back, stretching and contorting in a way that suggested he was maneuvering to put his arm around her, but it never quite got there. Finally, at a particularly suspenseful part, the girl swimming unaware, the monster lurking just below the surface. She grasped his forearm on the armrest between them. He put his other hand, his right one, on top of hers. They were holding hands.

His hand was clammy. But so was hers.

He finally managed to get his arm there. On the back of her seat, resting on the rough red upholstery itching his arm, scarcely touching her shoulder at first, gradually letting it settle into place until it could be said to be actually around her. Half an hour later, his shoulder was throbbing, his whole arm numb and tingly.

As for her, she had a crick in her neck from straining to maintain a position that was not too close, not too far, not too sweaty or heavy. She had a headache as well.

Neither of them had ever felt more wonderful.

The scariness of the movie never took root. They were too busy positioning their own bodies, reining in their own galloping hearts, feeling their own tinglings and stirrings and roilings and arousals.

After a while, something a little too close to tedium began to set in. He knew it was time. He licked his lips. She had decided the same thing at the same time and her face was turned, her eyes closed, her mouth waiting. The warm, moist touch of the faces at this moment was the most foreign and frightening and delicious sensation they'd ever felt.

The movie ended, the lights came up, but still they lingered, remaining in their seats holding hands, exchanging dopey glances, feeling blissfully mindless, clammy and throbbing. Filled with anxious anticipation of what they couldn't imagine would be next. They might have been alone, having long since forgotten others were in the theater.

A rude voice hollered from a few rows back. "Hey, Huffman! You gonna take her home to meet Killer George?"

The voice shouted Huffman's name a couple more times. Huffman didn't turn.

Gracie did. She looked back at Bowersox, then back again to Henry.

"It's a long story," he said, grimacing as though he'd stepped on a marble.

After Bowersox had given up and everyone was gone, Gracie and Huffman strolled hand-in-hand up through the popcorn and wrapper rubble. In the back row a kid was sweeping, knocking the broom handle against the seats, *boom, boom, boom.*

Now what? "Want to get something to eat?" he said.

"I'm not really hungry," she said.

"Shall I take you home?" he said.

"*No.*" She frowned. He was perplexed. He suspected he understood, but he wasn't sure. It might have only been hope.

They stopped outside, under the marquee. Down the block across Main, Siebert's' dark windows caught the reflection of the streetlight in front of the courthouse.

"We can't go to my place," she said. "Mrs. Long would have a fit."

"Yeah." He had picked her up at her boarding house, only a few blocks from his own place on Hastings Street, up on the south side of town. "We could go to my house," he said. "I guess."

She squeezed his hand and smiled. He warned her his father was there, that the place was a mess, that his father was a semi-invalid, and wasn't too good at picking up after himself. She said she'd be happy to clean up after him.

You won't be happy to clean up his shitty pants, he thought.

Luckily they were spared. As soon as they walked in, he breathed deeply, and although what he smelled wasn't pleasant, traces of stale sweat, faint mildew and old shoes, he was relieved by the absence of any hint of shit. His father was in his wheelchair in front of the television beneath the glare of the overhead light; he hadn't turned on a lamp. "Hi, Pop," he said.

Martha Raye was on, *Your Show of Shows.*.

"This is Gracie." He almost said, *my girlfriend*, then, checking himself, was going to say *my friend*, but ended up repeating, simply, "Gracie."

"I heard you the first time," his father grumbled from a phlegmy throat.

"How do you do, Mr. Huffman," she said.

His father said nothing and frowned. His eyes quickly slipped from Gracie's face, wandering rudely to her chest, then down to her belly and below, then back up to her bosom. Huffman detected a flush sprouting on her cheeks, and he glared at his father, his fat face unctuous and greasy, his hair slick and dirty. There were stains of unknown origin, although one looked suspiciously like grape jam, or oil, on his shirt, the buttons of which were misaligned. Huffman wished he'd cleaned him up.

"What are you watching, Pop?"

"Television," he said. Martha Raye was singing. The picture was not good.

Huffman adjusted the rabbit ears, and his father's attention clamped down once again on the picture. Huffman picked up a plate, an overturned cup and some miscellaneous, assorted wrappers and crumbs from the floor near his father's wheelchair and removed a stack of old newspapers from the sofa. "Want to watch Martha Raye?" he said to Gracie.

She frowned. "Where's your room?"

It was upstairs, where a wheelchair couldn't climb. It had been his parents' room when he was growing up, George and Elsie's. Huffman had taken it over after George's fall from the ladder, at the same time his father had moved into the little bedroom on the first floor that had been Huffman's—the same room that Huffman, as a child, had shared with his older cousin, Oscar, right up until his arrest.

His room was neat and clean, a little dusty perhaps, but not disastrously so. Even the air smelled better. It was dark, at the back of the house where the streetlamp on the corner didn't reach. He turned on the little lamp on the dresser. There was not a chair in the room, nothing on which to sit but the bed.

Gracie was a good girl, but she'd never felt this way before. Nor had she ever gone all the way—she had no intention of doing so before she was married—but she'd had some experience, some romantic encounters, with a boy from Erie named Alex, a boy she'd nearly loved. Huffman had more experience. There'd been Libby Matson, older, overweight and needy, when he was only thirteen, and there'd been Larry Allgeier's girlfriend's sister when he was a little older. There were always girls when you needed them, if you knew where to look, but they were not *nice* girls. He would not expect a *nice* girl to go all the way. And Gracie, he knew, *was* a nice girl. Really, all he wanted was to hold her—that would be enough. He'd never felt quite this way before.

Despite her inexperience she knew a few things. One thing led to another.

Afterwards, he apologized. "Jeeze," he said. "I'm sorry."

"Oh, don't worry. It'll come out. I can hold my pocketbook in front of it."

"I'll get something to wipe it off with."

"Really, don't bother."

"It's no bother." He went to the bathroom for a wash cloth, came back and helped her wipe away the stain on the front of her skirt. It didn't do much good. They laughed about it. "You can just say you spilled your milk."

"Right," she said. "No use crying over that."

They cuddled in the shadows on the bed. Through the window came the mesmerizing sounds of the crickets, and, from the marshes over by the railyard, the more distant sounds of bullfrogs in the night air. They lay entangled without discomfort. He'd never been more at peace. She felt as though she were floating on a magic carpet.

They heard a thump and a crash downstairs. His father yelled, "Elsie!"

Gracie frowned.

"Elsie! *Elsie!*"

Huffman sighed. Something began to gnaw at him, that nagging chore left undone, something beginning to peck its way out of its shell. "Who's Elsie?" she said.

"My mother. He does this all the time. He's always calling her."

"I thought your mother was gone."

"She is. She has been. She's been gone fifteen years or more, but who's counting?"

"*Elsie! Else!*"

"Gone where?"

"God only knows." Her hand, which had been caressing his chest, fell still. He felt his heart come up to beat against it. "She took off. It was a long time ago."

He recited: "There was this air show down at the fairgrounds, barnstorming pilots and all that. We went down one afternoon, then Mom went down again next day, by herself. There was this one pilot who had a smile like a beacon—he was all teeth, I swear. Well, it seems Mom was smitten with him." Smitten. There it was again: *smitten.* "So she went down again, next day, and that time she never came back."

"Really? She just took off? Disappeared?"

"Yes. It seems she'd taken off—no pun intended—with that pilot guy, whatever his name was, *Ace* something."

"Why, that's awful. She just left you to take care of your dad?"

"That might have been the biggest reason. She couldn't be bothered with him."

"That's just awful. What's the matter with him, anyhow?"

"He fell off a ladder and broke his back." He took a deep breath. He felt as though he were beginning to tumble downhill in a rock slide.

He went on. "Of course, that was after Mom cracked him on the head with a big old iron skillet."

She stared at him, frowning through the shadows. "My goodness," she said. "That poor man."

"Yeah." *Killer George.* "I guess I might as well tell you the rest."

"There's more?"

"Sure. Isn't there always?" He put his hand behind his head. She lived in Hartsgrove now. Everyone in Hartsgrove knew. Sooner or later she would, too. Better now, from him, than later, from someone else. It seemed a necessary first step on a journey back to where he'd been only moments before, at peace. In love.

He told her first about his cousin, Oscar, who was older, nearly his father's age, who lived with them when Huffman was little, how they'd shared a room. What he remembered about Oscar was that he trapped rabbits for their furs, hung the skins to dry on the back porch—Huffman to this day couldn't sit on the porch without smelling the scent of dried blood and rotting meat. The back porch overlooked the railyard. He told her about the night the woman who worked there in the signal tower was killed, such a night, sirens blaring the whole night long, every light in town blazing. And how Oscar, the night watchman at the glass plant nearby, had been arrested for the murder, tried, convicted and put to death in the electric chair a couple of years later. Insisting to the end he didn't do it.

Henry believed him; he didn't think it could have been his cousin. Many in the town never believed it was Oscar either—some blamed his father instead, his mother among that number. Hence the all-out brawl one day, the heavy skillet, the damaged brain. She'd served six months for assault, and after her release she had no inclination to take care of the man she suspected, the man she'd left addled. Huffman recited his story as though reciting a familiar verse. Not too long afterward, he said, she'd barnstormed off with the pilot. *Ace* something.

Gracie by now was sitting up on the bed. Her skin had turned cold, her face had hardened. "Who was the woman in the signal tower?" she said, though she knew. She wanted to hear him say it. "What was her name?"

"Let me think. Watson, maybe, Wilson?"

"It was Wilson," she said. "It was Lucy Wilson."

* * *

"I can see where it might muss up her hair a little bit," Radaker said, never looking up from the board he was measuring, "but it ain't like *you* killed her aunt."

"Might as well be," Huffman said. "You should have seen her face."

"That's all water over the damn bridge. I imagine she'll get over it."

"I don't know," said Huffman.

In the empty little store on Main Street where Radaker was building new cabinets, Huffman sat in the corner on a bucket of spackle, his necktie drooping loose. A low afternoon sun through the storefront window made the fine powder of sawdust glitter on the floor. Gracie wouldn't answer his calls. Mrs. Long said she'd just stepped out, or was sleeping, or had her hands full and couldn't come to the phone.

Radaker said, "What was it—twenty years ago? I can barely even remember it."

"Eighteen," Huffman said. "But who's counting?"

"Well, she ain't, I guess. Ancient history." Radaker placed the board in the miter box and commenced his cut.

"Is it?" Was it?

It wasn't. It was fresh again, newly installed in the here and now. Something—someone—had brought it back around. Made it as though it had happened only yesterday. Something—someone—had wanted to make certain it didn't go away, wasn't forgotten, wanted to ensure that the sins of his family were never far from the sunlight.

Radaker blew sawdust from the end of the board. "What are the odds?" he asked. "Here you are just walking around minding your own business and here this girl just up and walks into your store and you fall for her, and she turns out to be the niece of the woman your cousin killed. Or who they say your cousin killed anyways, who they arrested for it and who they claim done it. And even if he didn't do it, it didn't make much never-mind, since he went to the chair for it anyways, even if he didn't do it." His face was getting redder, talking himself into a corner. "Small world," he said, and let it go at that.

Huffman said, "Do you believe there's a God?"

"Why, hell yes," Radaker said. "Just look at this here board." He held it out, beheld it, a Holy Grail with splinters. "This was just an acorn at one time, a little bitty acorn no bigger'n your little toe. How can anybody look at this and believe there ain't no God?"

"I guess so," said Huffman. He was afraid his friend was right. "And I guess He must have one hell of a sense of humor."

* * *

Down the corridor, call lights were calling. Bursting out of 322, Mrs. Carrier spotted Elva and Gracie at the nurses' station. "Ladies! There's feces all over in here!"

"Oh, shit," Elva said softly, and began to giggle. Gracie knew Elva expected her to giggle along, like two kids in church, but Gracie couldn't. She did not possess the means at this point to muster up so much as a chuckle.

Mrs. Carrier's angry face was closing in fast. "May I ask *why* you are just standing here? Three lights blinking, and Mrs. Grubb is a mess."

"Yes," Gracie said.

"Yes, *what*?" said Mrs. Carrier.

"Yes, you may ask why we're just standing here."

As Mrs. Carrier's face began to balloon in shock, Elva intervened. "We were just on our way—we're going now, aren't we Gracie? We were just on our way, but Gracie's terribly upset. We just had to take a minute."

"You may be upset on your own time!"

"Oh, shut up," Gracie said, and headed toward Mr. Stockdale in 317.

She could feel the horrified eyes of both the older ladies watching her walk away. Mr. Stockdale had to use the toilet, couldn't get out of bed by himself, and didn't want the bedpan. He would sooner die than allow a young nurse to view the fruits of his bladder and bowels. As she eased him across the room, she heard Elva snap at Mrs. Carrier, "Oh, shut up," and, a second later, she heard her say, "Can't you see she has a broken heart?"

Her heart? Broken? No.

Elva was wrong. Perhaps it ought to be, certainly. A love she'd felt— *yes*, however brief, it had felt like love, like real love—had turned to ashes, true, and her heart was sick, certainly—but broken? No. Her heart felt more like a stone than a fragile thing of flesh and blood, and stones were not easily broken.

"It's not like *he* killed your aunt," Elva had told her.

That's where she was wrong again. That's exactly what it was like. Perhaps Henry didn't kill her, but it was *like* he did. Gracie saw the resemblance between Henry and his father. And then she remembered the picture in the paper her mother had pointed to when she was a little girl, *this is the man who killed your aunt*. Oscar, the name. She remembered that face quite clearly, as though she'd seen it only yesterday, and it was the same face, the same pasty, white, doughy-bland face as George's—the same face as Henry's. It was the last face, the last *thing*, her Aunt Lucy had ever seen.

Mr. Stockdale, wispy hair, spotted gray skull, gave a sudden flinch and whimper.

Gracie recoiled. She let go of his arm, seeing the bruises where her fingers had dug in, leaving their spiteful marks like burns.

* * *

Then came the fire. Gracie had quit her job, packed her bags, and was ready to leave. She still hadn't spoken to Henry. She'd evaded his calls, which had slowed to a trickle then stopped.

Huffman had given up. He'd resigned himself to never seeing her again.

But he did see her again, one last time.

She was standing almost directly across from him, among a crowd of people watching, most of whom he knew, neighbors of some degree or other. They'd all come to gape in awe at the flames.

The smoke galloped up in big, black, rollicking billows from the little house on Hastings Street, into the pristine blue sky of the summer afternoon. The crackling, popping, hissing noises were louder even than the occasional exclamations, the intermittent, excited chatter from the throng gathered around, spectators, watching rapt, mesmerized, quiet. They'd gathered in front, in the street, and all around the little house as well, far back from the searing heat, nearly to the gully that bordered the backyard, beyond which was the railyard where the signal tower no longer stood. Further beyond were the ruins of the old glass plant, the plant where cousin Oscar had been the watchman on that night so long ago.

The men of the Hartsgrove Volunteer Fire Department trained torrents of water on the flames, to little effect, mostly watching, mostly spectators. Smokey Bowersox was one of the volunteers. He stood back by the pumper, taller than the rest, with something that looked to Huffman like a phantom of a grin on his face.

Radaker was late to the scene. Spotting Huffman, he approached, watching the fire, making his way through the on-lookers, slack-jawed and frowning in awe at the writhing, beating violence of the flames.

When he reached his friend, he looked around, taking in all the gawking faces. "Ain't that Gracie over there?"

Huffman only nodded.

Gracie's eyes were fixed on the fire, her face unreadable.

Radaker looked around again. "Where's George?" he said. "Where's your pop?"

Huffman put his hand on the back of his neck. He nodded at the conflagration.

"He ain't still—"

Huffman nodded again. His face was white, sweating with heat.

"Holy smoke," said Radaker.

Loretta Lynn at the Grand Ole Opry

Her daddy's daughter
raises her
formidable palm
up to Jesus first
then to her fans
under Ryman's spotlights
her ivory dress shimmers
like diamonds in the dew
her butter-bean voice sweeps
out to smooth my hair
kiss the crown of my head
breathe in deeply
the way I will
with my daughters
a decade from now
depths of faith
from Butcher Holler
How Great Thou Art
her voice breaks
as she rolls over
"Oh my God"
like holy waters
my heart halts
into a country fist
as I imagine her
whirling in circles
bare feet in wet grass
beneath Johnny Cash's
window at 3 a.m.
an Appalachian apparition

Waffles, INCaffeinated

I'm somewhere trendy and empty
in a dying downtown on its sixth try
at urban renewal. If you watch the news,
every time a new breakfast place opens
you'd swear the ghost of Andrew Carnegie
came back like a robber baron Jesus
to heal our postindustrial wounds.
And here I am, the only person eating
in a place that easily seats a hundred,
waiting on a goat cheese omelet,
unsure about the future.

Karen Whittington Nelson

Though I Will It Otherwise

The gelding was never the same after the mare
colicked and died. And when he too passed,
the herd dwindled to the pony and me. The
little horse wore solitude like a sour blanket
and bonded with me to ease her loneliness.
We commiserated in a silent language,
soothed one another with touch,
shared the musky scents of sweat, manure
and weariness as I mucked her stall.

We swallowed our sorrows, the pony's less bitter
when stirred into a steaming mash. For me,
chocolate, dark and bittersweet. Gradually,
the pragmatic pony rallied; her expectations
shriveled to the dimensions of her new reality.
I snipped away at mine, took in a tuck here and there.

In the evening, the pony beds down in the stable
with a full belly; I lie alone in the dim bedroom,
read the ceiling, toss and search for comfort
in the clumpy bed. Though I will it otherwise,

I'm aware of the persistent scent of *him*
lingering upon the fallow pillow. I whisper,
then swallow his name, kick aside blankets,
clamber from the bed and tiptoe down the hall
to count my sleeping children.

Moonlight diffuses the shadows on the beds.
I allow my fingertips to kiss each childish outline,
hold my breath and wait for the gentle stir of blankets
to rise and greet my touch.

Mincemeat

Overriding Mom's objections, Daddy closed his barber shop in Duncan Falls, Ohio, and moved us to his family's farm in Morgan County on what locals had dubbed Heathen Ridge. At twelve, I wasn't any happier than Mom about the sudden upheaval—or the change in lifestyle. On the Ridge, modern conveniences consisted of electricity and a telephone connection known as a party line. For entertainment, Mom had her radio, and I listened in on the neighbors' calls when no one was paying attention.

Early the following summer, Daddy and his sister Joyce purchased a couple of shoats to fatten up and butcher in the fall. As a farm-girl-in-training, I was in charge of the slop bucket, a metal pail filled with kitchen scraps, outdated foodstuff, and no-soap dishwater. Every evening, I tossed the fragrant mess into the food trough while Daddy forked fresh straw into the pen and filled their water trough.

Aunt Joyce, who lived in McConnelsville, stopped by now and then to make sure her investment was taking on sufficient poundage. Mom's tolerance of her sister-in-law had maxed out years ago; Daddy had big pockets for Joyce; not so much for Mom and me.

One snappy evening in November, I was returning from slopping duty when I spotted my aunt's car in the twin ruts that passed for a driveway. Through the deepening dusk, I watched her fill a bucket at the coal shed, lug it to the pigpen, and dump it over the fence.

Sizeable by now, the two porkers left off slurping at the trough and attacked the blue-black mineral like it was Christmas candy. Razor-sharp incisors sliced through the coal faster than I could bite an apple. Dusting her hands in satisfaction, she spotted me standing there with my mouth hanging open. "Don't worry. Coal is good for pigs."

When my aunt's taillights topped the rise above the house, Mom appeared at the door. "What's she up to now?"

At the phrase "bucketful of coal," Mom grabbed a cardigan and a flashlight and headed toward the hog pen. "A little bit of coal is one thing, but a bucketful?"

Hustling to match her stride, I ventured a comment. "Maybe they won't eat it all at once." She gave me a look I could read even in the dark.

At the pen, Mom's flashlight beam revealed a diminishing pile of coal. One pig had ingested its fill and bedded down, but the other continued to pulverize chunk after chunk, powerful molars performing what seemed an impossible task. We grabbed tomato stakes, hoping to discourage the pig with sharp jabs, but the wooden sticks weren't long enough. I was swinging onto the fence to get a better reach when Mom jerked on my shirt. "You want those teeth chewing on you?"

We threw rocks and shouted, but the gorging continued to the last morsel. Then the pig joined its mate in the lean-to shelter.

That's when Daddy showed up. He'd spent the day barbering in the small town of Waterford, having found that actual money was required to survive on the farm. I told him what I'd told Mom.

"That much," he mused, "and you say it's all gone? Well, they do like coal."

The next morning, I followed Daddy outside. One hog rooted around the frosty ground; the other lay motionless in the lean-to, its belly distended.

"Foundered," Daddy muttered.

I didn't have to ask what he meant. The gluttonous pig was just as sunk from its surfeit as the *Titanic* from its intake of water.

A slaughtered animal, I'd learned when we beheaded the rowdy young roosters in our flock, had to be bled out immediately. Nothing could erase the sight of those headless adolescents running hither and yon, blood spurting from their empty necks.

So, instead of potential ham and pork chops we were looking at a useless carcass. Back in the kitchen, Daddy called his sister to give her the news. Mom beat six eggs to a froth and dumped them into the sizzling skillet, message loud and clear: Joyce owes somebody a pig.

She and Uncle Robert came wheeling in soon after. Seeing the results of her handiwork lying sprawled where Daddy had dragged it out of reach of its sibling, my aunt pulled a tissue from her pocket. Daddy, thoroughly miffed seconds before, softened at his sister's sniffling and offered a generous solution: "We'll split the other hog and call it even," he said.

Joyce blew her nose and stooped to get a better look at the deceased. "But this is *your* hog, Raymond. See the spot over the right eye? My hog is in the pen."

Even Daddy was having trouble with that level of logic, and Mom's eyes narrowed to blue slits, but Daddy's hand on her arm forestalled the boilover. Throughout the exchange, Robert, tall and skeletal and long-experienced in his wife's tactics, said nothing.

Conceding defeat, Daddy gathered the shreds of his manliness. "You womenfolk go in the house. Robert and I will take care of things here."

Normally, Mom and Joyce would have gone to the kitchen and maintained a façade of civility over coffee. Today, jaw set like a mutineer's, Mom marched toward the house sans word or gesture. Joyce could stand in the cold or return to her car.

Joyce chose the car.

I hung back while Daddy hitched up the workhorse Twyla to a skid and watched each man grab a pair of legs and hoist the carcass onto the conveyance. Twyla snorted and flattened her ears but calmed down when Daddy held the reins beneath her chin and led her forward.

Slowly, the funereal procession advanced, with Uncle Robert bringing up the rear, head bowed as though in benediction. They disappeared where the hayfield dropped into a gully that harbored the refuse of generations. I high-tailed it to the house, as the ubiquitous red clay welcomed its latest inhabitant.

That winter, the anticipated sizzle of fresh side and tenderloin failed to materialize in the farmhouse kitchen, as did the fragrance of homemade sausage enliven our breakfasts. My aunt, however, didn't ignore us entirely. When the school bus dropped me off one blustery December evening, there on the kitchen table, resting in a white enamel dishpan, was a boiled pig skull with bits of skin and meat clinging to brow and cheeks and jowls, awaiting me to pick it clean.

Hogshead, I was to discover, is the key ingredient in mincemeat. When combined with apples and raisins and spices and baked in a flaky crust, it becomes what some folks consider a delicacy. As appealing as the pastry smelled, I had to pass. All I could see when I looked at the pie were empty eye sockets and teeth locked in a lipless grin.

Linda Mills Woolsey

Aunt Mildred at the Mangle

From the safety of the doorway I watched
her strong arms wrangle cloth into the mangle's
grim mouth as I stood there, small, tight-fisted,
trying so hard to be good. If to labor is to pray,
I know now her work was prayer itself, intent,
unhurried, each blued damask tablecloth,
each smoothed sheet or polished sleeve
a stay against confusion.

Back then, being so much fussed at, we knew
ourselves much loved. Warned of dangers all
around, in childhood's house mangle was a noun
of order and a verb of mayhem. The machines
of household comfort worked by searing heat,
severing blades, bone-crushing rollers. Even
the sewing machine, prim in its oak shrine
wielded a piercing power.

Danger beckoned us from all the mangonels
and trebuchets of housework as our eager fingers
brushed the switches and dials of ordinary doom.
The mangle—its padded drum like a bandaged
arm—defied the reach of our ambition. So we
hunkered under the Singer, pumped the treadle's
iron lace fast and faster till we felt the needle's
leap and stab deep in our rascal hearts.

We still believed in cartoon peril, having seen
Wile E. Coyote crushed flat by the steam roller
a thousand times, only to pop up and stagger off
with a wobbly grin. Though my breath caught
each time her fingers drew close to the mangle's
maw, I believed in a world where she could never
die. Now lost, she returns to me in a Vermeer light
hallowing every ordinary task.

I want to run back, into the room of long ago, rest
my hand on her shoulder just one more time, ask her
a thousand questions, let her strong hands guide me
through this day's work of making do in the house
of loss. It's my turn to learn her courage and to dare
the ordinary dangers of each newly dampened day
as it comes, waiting to be pressed, folded, put to use
in the ordinary offices of love.

Making cider

for Ted Scarpino

A crisp stew
of sweet, tart, bitter.
Fuji Gala Empire
Macintosh Winesap Liberty
Cortland Newton Crabapple.

An assembly line's artless party.
Bob and Dennis flanking water tubs,
excise bruises,
toss apples from the first
to splash in the second.

Jan and Sue loft the washed,
into the hopper,
a shark's mouth
of steel teeth,
set over a wooden spindle
turning apples to pulp.

(a dish above the open top,
or everyone is pulp sprayed.)

Dave and Ann fit rice sacks for pulp and juice
into steel banded oak baskets.
Full baskets slide to the collecting pan.

Rosalie operates the press,
folds rice sack over pulp,
covers with the press plate,
tightens the screw.

Juice streams down the pan,
set below a tapered end.
Ted eyes fast filling jugs.
A job for the vigilant.

Pulp for goats.
Juice for folks.

Harvest Salad

Greens must be massaged.
Sara shows me how, her
calloused garden hands
softening in olive oil.
We work the kale in small batches
leaf by leaf over the hand painted stoneware bowl,
mixing in shiitakes from the market
gently sautéed with purple garlic
an old neighbor, years ago,
taught us to grow.
Sara laughs, musing at how tempted we were
that first year to dig the bulbs too soon.
To dig when their flowers first popped
their lavender pompons
and the honeybees came,
and the hummingbirds came.
But we had been warned that
to avoid sharp and bitter garlic,
we must wait for the flowers
to fade, and dry,
and fall.
Wait for the green thick leaf blades to begin
yellowing,
and withering.
Only then is the harvest
rich and full-flavored,
mature and enduring.

The Stream a River

Blue drains from the afternoon, leaves behind a hint of day.
The frost moon's gaze cool and detached,
the air breathy, dry and crisp, sweet with decay.
I rake leaves down the slope toward the wood's edge;
the sound mimics the ebb and flow of water, *whoosh . . . whoosh.*
The leaves become a stream, the stream a river.
My rake dredges up fragile remains, mummified mice, snails
and alabaster bones, varied and mysterious as the gifts
left behind by the Muskingum, scattered across the bank
below my grandparents' house.

The rake handle snags my gloves; the work grows tiresome.
My reach becomes shorter, lighter. I hear water lapping
against the hull of Grandpa's leaky rowboat, *whoosh . . . whoosh.*
The boat bumps against the dock, its silvered planks
held above the water line by rusted, sealed drums that vibrate
with soft, deep thunder, my innards with their soothing rumble.
Beer bottles trapped inside the flat-bottomed boat
slosh about in the shallow water, clink cheers
and rub their labels against the hull, until naked and nameless,
they'll slip overboard, destined to be reincarnated as river-polished
        amber.

Evening stars appear in the sky and twinkle, a garland of party lights
warming up—or perhaps, sputtering out. The leaves lie gathered
and uncomplaining, the river shimmers like a silk ribbon, gurgles
like a sleepy infant.

Grandma guides my hands. I pierce a needle through a tender shell
gleaned from the riverbank, string kitchen twine through the prettiest
    ones.
She ties the necklace loosely around my neck, the shells cool
and chalky against my skin. When they jostle one another,
only I hear their voices, soft as whispering castanets, *shh . . . shh.*
I hide their secrets under my tongue, not yet having any of my own.

Mockingbird

Your body tried to die
at least a dozen times
then you shot out
of the world when
no one was watching. Thief
who stole you must've got
a handful of fury, that's how
hard you hung on. You kept
that pacemaker ticking
under your skin long after
the warranty expired, wanting
more, next meal, next movie.
In Pittsburgh, while we waited
to see a heart specialist
I pushed your wheelchair
through the Carnegie, past
Segal's mummified tightrope walker,
skeletal Giacometti figures,
gaunt, grief-bound,
their downcast eyes. Not you.
Every gorgeous day was
a gorgeous day. You had to
repeat it, like something
in you took flight, like it was
something worth fighting for.
A gorgeous day.
Your mockingbird soul now gone
won't stop calling out
in the dazzling sun. It's on

the tallest branch
of the tallest pine.
I can't see it,
but it's there, singing.

Bear

A teddy bear is not alive.
I know this, but it's hard to remember
when life's scars crisscross my bear's eyes
and her fur has gone gray
with grime that repeated washings can't remove.
It's hard to remember now
because my bear stood beside me
long before I met my husband,
and she will stand beside me
when my love is gone, when the disease inside him
makes its final victory.
And I'll wish my love had stuffing inside
so he could live forever.

Black Feathers

The day President Kennedy was assassinated, Joey Johnson walked home from school. It was a gray afternoon, and a cold wind blew. Joey walked home every day because the bus cost a dime and he usually didn't have it. When he did, he hated spending it on the bus. With two dimes he could get a hamburger at the White Light and heap on ketchup, mustard, and relish.

On this day he walked home with Donnie Wood, who also did not have a dime. They both lived in the east end, the poor part of town. The shortest route from the high school was to walk straight up First Avenue past a sprawling tobacco warehouse, a couple of gas stations, a drugstore, the shoe factory where Joey's mother worked, a small grocery, the VFW hall, and a scattering of small houses set close to the sidewalk. There were no trees.

Today Joey steered Donnie up Maple Avenue, a longer but nicer route, a residential street where trees grew between the sidewalk and the street, and the mowed lawns were large. Many of the houses were brick. The trees were mostly bare now, and wet leaves piled up in the gutters. Today he wanted to walk past something nice.

"It's weird," Joey said. "I feel like someone's died."

Donnie burst out laughing. "Someone *has* died, you dipstick."

Joey didn't laugh. "That's not what I'm saying. It's not just that somebody has died. It's *like* somebody has died. It's a feeling. A feeling in the air. Like the whole world just slipped off its chassis or something. That's what I'm saying."

Donnie shrugged. A truck loaded with tobacco rumbled past. The annual opening of the market was next Monday.

"They shot him in the head. There was blood all over Jackie Kennedy," Donnie said.

"How do you know that?" Joey asked.

"Sally Smith had a transistor radio last period. Mrs. Collins let her turn it on for the whole period," Donnie said.

Joey put his hands in his jacket pockets. The wind felt cold.

"Maybe the communists killed him," Joey said.

"Some people say Kennedy was a communist," Donnie said.

"That's stupid," Joey said.

Donnie lifted his feet and clicked his heels hard on the sidewalk, trying to make sparks fly. Like a lot of the guys from the east end, he wore heel plates. The sharp clacking noise gave the wearer a feeling of power. The school had banned them, claiming they damaged the floors, but boys learned to walk on the sides of their soles when the principal was around.

Joey had only one pair of shoes, Converse high tops. You couldn't put metal plates on anything but hard heels and soles.

"I wonder how they shot him," Joey said.

"The radio said he was in a convertible with the top down," Donnie said.

Joey imagined himself in the crowd, seeing the gunman and jumping in front of Kennedy to take the bullet.

Donnie saw a hand of tobacco lying in the gutter and he picked it up. It was intact, neatly wrapped. It reminded Joey of a girl's golden brown ponytail.

"I can take this to the warehouse and sell it," Donnie said.

"I've heard that. Is it true? They'll buy just a few hands?"

"I heard it, too. I don't know. I aim to find out."

Joey's stomach hurt from hunger. Lunch in the cafeteria was $1.25 a week, and this week he didn't have it, so he didn't get lunch. A few weeks ago his mother passed out at work and she hadn't been back. The doctor said she had to rest. Next summer Joey would turn sixteen, so he had been thinking he might quit school and get a job.

"What did they have in the cafeteria today?" Joey asked.

"Fish. It's Friday," Donnie said.

"I ate at the White Light," Joey lied.

Joey didn't tell Donnie about not having lunch money. Donnie was a good friend, but Joey couldn't talk to him about some things. Such as it felt *like* someone died. Such as how his mother was sick. Or how when Joey arrived at school that morning, he saw an apple core lying in the grass. It was fresh and he picked it up and slipped it into the pocket of his jacket. He went into the boys' bathroom and rinsed it under the tap. He ate it, picking from his mouth the stem and seeds. He imagined that one of the pretty girls had eaten that apple as her father drove her to school in something like a Chevy Impala or a Buick Riviera. He tried to imagine which pretty girl it was, his mouth being where hers had been. He would never tell Donnie that, or how he had thought about it all day.

Nobody in the east end was rich, but Joey was downright poor. He knew it.

TV? They didn't have one. Radio? It was broken. Shirts? Three t-shirts and two with buttons. Pants? One brown to dress up and then his jeans. Father? Left when Joey was in first grade. One younger brother, J.C. You might as well call their house a shack.

"I wonder what it's like to live there," Joey said, nodding toward a white brick home.

"Aw, man," Donnie said. "I bet they eat chicken or steak every night. And pie and ice cream. I bet they have a color TV. Stereo. All that stuff."

"I bet some of them have dogs," Joey said.

"Linda Lovett has a Cocker Spaniel," Donnie said. "She lives along here. I saw her walking it one day."

"I'd like to have me a German Shepherd police dog," Joey said.

Donnie veered into the gutter to kick at a pile of leaves.

"There must be a lot about it on TV," Joey said.

"About what?"

"Kennedy."

"Yeah, I guess."

"I might go down to Boy's Club tonight to watch it," Joey said.

"I might go, too. Shoot some pool," Donnie said.

They passed a funeral home. Joey turned up the collar of his jacket.

"I wonder what kind of funeral they'll have," Joey said.

"Man, you're really thinking about that," Donnie said.

"I know it. I know I am."

They turned right at Wood Street, crossed the railroad tracks, and climbed the hill. Joey welcomed the climb. It warmed him up. Donnie was still carrying his hand of tobacco. They crossed First Avenue into the east end neighborhood. Donnie turned down his street saying he might see Joey later at the Boy's Club.

Joey passed the long brick housing project building where his mother refused to live, even though they qualified. Joey thought it looked okay. As he walked, the houses got smaller, dingier.

When he neared his house, second from the end, he inhaled the smell of frying chicken. He lifted his nose like a dog sniffing the air. He took another breath, a deep one. There was no mistaking it. Nothing else smelled like that. His empty stomach growled. What he would give to be eating there.

He wondered which house it was. It was growing dusk now, and the closer he got to his own house, the stronger the smell. It was the fullest, most satisfying, the most beautiful smell he had ever smelled.

Uncle Jack's pick-up was parked in front. Uncle Jack lived out in the country and worked on a farm. Joey's brother J.C. was shooting marbles in the bare dirt of the tiny yard. Joey walked through the door and was enveloped in the smell. It was coming from his own kitchen.

Uncle Jack appeared with a spatula in his hand.

"Is that fried chicken?" Joey cried.

"Close to it. That and a pot of white beans with a piece of salt pork. Your mama isn't feeling too good so I came on by to cook up some supper for you boys."

Joey looked wide-eyed at the stove where an iron skillet with a mismatched lid popped and sizzled.

"Oh, boy!" he cried.

Uncle Jack laughed.

Joey saw a pellet gun on the counter and picked it up.

"Remember your rules now. Don't put your finger on the trigger and don't point it at anybody."

"It's just a pellet gun," Joey said.

"A gun's a gun," Uncle Jack said.

"Yes sir," Joey answered.

"This will be done pretty soon," Uncle Jack said. "Better get J.C. in."

From the bedroom, Joey heard his mother's voice.

He pushed open the door and said, "Hi, Mama."

She had the quilt pulled up to her chin. A small lamp on the floor beside the bed gave the only light, so she was lying mostly in shadow. The Bible was beside her.

Joey's chest tightened. "How come you're reading the Bible?" he asked.

"Just some comfort, I reckon. They shot the President, Joey." Her voice sounded weak.

"I know. They announced it at school. I keep thinking about it."

"I didn't vote for him, but now I wish I had," his mother said. She sighed. "It's too late now."

"I heard that one of the teachers cried," Joey said.

"I shed a tear myself," his mother said. "I couldn't help it."

"Well," Joey said.

"You go on and eat now. Uncle Jack has something for you and J.C."

"Aren't you going to eat?"

"I'm not hungry today, honey. You go on now. I'll get mine later."

"Okay, Mama," Joey said.

Joey called J.C. in and they washed their hands at the sink and dried them on their shirts. They all sat at the table. It was a folding table with a red plastic table cloth and metal folding chairs. The pot of beans was on the table.

Uncle Jack set down a plastic plate piled high with golden fried pieces. He set glasses before the boys and poured half a Coke for each. He gave each a paper plate.

Joey took a breath. "That smells so darn good," he said.

"I want a drumstick," J.C. said.

"These here chickens just have one kind of piece," Uncle Jack said. "They're real skinny, so you got to take a few pieces. Get all the meat off the bone."

Uncle Jack was right. There was just a little dark meat on each piece, but Joey's favorite part was the crust anyway. Joey ate six of the little pieces and three helpings of white beans, but he was still hungry.

J.C. burped from the Coke and said, "Excuse me."

"Did you hear about Kennedy?" Joey asked Uncle Jack..

Uncle Jack said, "I heard it on the radio in my truck. They said it was an ex-Marine that did it. Seems like you can't trust nobody."

"A Marine? Durn." Joey had thought about joining the Marines when he turned eighteen.

"When I was at the store, I heard the tobacco market might not open Monday," Uncle Jack said. "I have a floor job, too."

"Yeah? Are you going to be a grader?"

"Naw, just forklift work. Hauling baskets. You have to get certified to be a grader. They make good money, though."

Joey liked talking with men like Uncle Jack about jobs and stuff like that.

J.C. pulled something from his mouth and looked at it. It was a tiny metal chunk. He put it in his pocket.

The pieces of fried chicken disappeared quickly. Tiny bones were heaped on the paper plates.

After they ate, Uncle Jack washed the pot and skillet, and Joey dried them. Uncle Jack poured the grease down the sink.

Joey's mother always said not to do that, but Joey didn't say anything. Joey put the paper plates in a stack. His mother reused them when she could.

Uncle Jack pulled a small can of Copenhagen from his hip pocket, took a pinch of snuff and placed it between his cheek and gum. Joey had tried it some but he hated the taste.

Joey asked Uncle Jack when Mama was going to get better.

Uncle Jack slid the can into his pocket and said, "Don't know, Joey. It might be a while yet."

Then he left. Joey wished he could go with him.

Joey took a paper plate with the last two pieces of the chicken into Mama's room, but she was asleep. He left it on the floor beside her bed. Maybe if she ate more she'd get better faster.

Joey sat on the plaid couch in the front room. J.C. tried to wrestle him onto the floor but he bumped heads with Joey and got mad. Joey pulled a *Life* magazine out of a wooden crate and sat down in one of the aluminum chairs. He thumbed through it, hoping to see a photo of Kennedy, but there wasn't one.

Joey heard a noise on the back porch. He pulled the door open and flicked on the porch light just in time to see a big rat crawl out of a cardboard box and scurry off the porch, its long hairless tail trailing it like a gray snake. He wanted to throw something at it, but he didn't have anything. Joey hadn't seen that box before, so he crossed the porch to look inside.

The box was stuffed with something black and glistening. For an instant he thought it was a fur coat. He gingerly put in his hand and felt feathers. He tilted the box to let the porch light shine in. It was feathers, all right, fistfuls of feathers, along with bird feet, globs of guts, and bird heads with yellow beaks and black, blank eyes.

He withdrew his hand and stared. His palm and fingers were smeared with blobs of bird doo and slimy innards. He felt in his stomach before it registered in his brain that Uncle Jack had shot a bunch of crows and fried them up for supper. Joey wiped his hand on his jeans.

The box seemed to spin in front of him, and there was a rumbling in his stomach. He turned his head and threw up, the spew of vomit splattering the porch.

"Shit," he said.

His throat burned. Still bent over, his hands on his knees, he spit and wiped his mouth on the back of his hand. He saw that his puke covered one entire shoe. He felt a flash of rage, blind, impotent, throat-searing rage, and he pulled off the shoe, stumbled into the yard, and flung it over the roof. He heard it thump on the street in front of his house.

Breathing hard, he sat down on the porch step. The only sound was his own breathing. There was no wind and the cold night air felt good on his face. The crickets and peepers of summer were gone now, so the autumn night was quiet. The long winter would be like that—silent. He thought about Kennedy. At least I'm alive, he thought. That's something. He remembered the apple core he ate that morning, how good it tasted. He thought of his mother. He would not let himself wonder if she was going to die.

In the kitchen he washed his hands and rinsed his mouth and filled a pan with water to slosh the vomit from the back porch. Then he limped in his one shoe back into the kitchen and out the front door.

He would have to find his other shoe and clean it off. It was the only pair he owned.

Bitter Supper

Words gather on the limbs of dead trees
          at the edge of a field. They rattle,
      click, coo, and caw. Years ago, I boasted,
told everyone I would be the richest man.

Today, I catch that black-feathered bird
          with my bare hands. I wring its neck,
      pluck its plumage, roast and baste it,
bring it to my lips. My father told me

I'd never have two nickels to rub together,
          as though that would propagate treasure,
      prosperity, moolah, gravy.
I could use a spoonful of gravy

to make this foul meal palatable,
          this dry breast, this withered wing,
      this shriveled leg. A crow is a liar
and a thief. I know the tough meat

of humiliation. I've seen entire sentences
          open their ravenous wings.
      They call out raucous and taunting,
echo over an unfinished meal.

Estonia. Many Years Hence . . .

My dear Baltic waves have conspired
    to take me and carry me away
    where peeling park benches are tired
    of keeping the secrets at bay.

Here charcoal and train station longing
    embitter the air of the town;
    the jetties run northward, prolonging
    the beach and the braided skyline.

We guzzled Estonian beer
    and feasted on local fare,
    and effortlessly, without ire
    I mentioned the Russian warfare.

"You sound like a frontline reporter,"
    Maxim said to me. "That's so plain.
    Your poems are simpler and shorter,
    your essays spell conflict and pain."

And Katya was stubbornly silent
    while stirring the thin amber slice
    of sunset. She hadn't lost her talent
    for noticing artifice.

We knew that this wasn't on purpose,
    we felt it within our hearts,
    yet saying those words was hurtful.
    We're different. Different. But how?

Our dear Baltic waves left us orphaned
     yet brought us the old salt taste
     of our Soviet childhood . . .
How can we be saved from ourselves?

Michael Comiskey

The Jews of Appalachia

No one knows precisely why they came here.
The early Jews of Appalachia, long since passed,
had motives known to God but lost to history.
Perhaps it should be no surprise or mystery,
though, that people so long shunned and outcast
landed here after wandering two thousand years:
this outcast region offered opportunities
presented by the region's major industries.
But, as elsewhere, finding few unprejudiced
employers, these itinerants, these dispossessed,
began their own establishments, little companies
that served their little prosperous communities.
They built and tended well-kept homes
and greatly prized hard work and education,
obeyed the law and paid their taxes.
As we all know, though, the fact is
they achieved despite genteel discrimination,
yet wished their neighbors undisturbed *shalom*.
Dispersed again now are the Sterns and Greensteins,
not by wind or edict but by shuttered mills and mines.
They've left behind born-again Churches of God
with six-pointed stars on their white-washed facades.

Appalachian Sonnet

The Appalachian Mountains are a sight to see,
from the Bald Mountains to the Long Range Mountains.
Every sight is breathtaking as you turn a blind eye
to the people who lived in these mountains for generations.
Every year their children go cold and hungry,
as the coal miners work long hours to pay the bills,
waiting for the day when they're told their mines are closed down,
now forced to find a job outside the experience of coal
that turned their lungs blacker and blacker and weaker and weaker
    with every breath.
They beg for government help and get turned away again and again.
And I fall for the empty promise I'm told at 18,
that I can thrive and grow within these mountains.
And now I'm 24 with a dead-end job that keeps me poor.
Therein lies the real beauty of the Appalachian Mountains.

Why I Have Clutter

Under my bed is a nest
that regret built.
I should have cleaned
it up years ago,
Dusted away the unsaid words.
Vacuumed up the promise,
unsaid but understood,
that I broke.
It's left a dent
in the carpet.
Each time I lift the bedspread,
vacuum purring, I stop.
Because it's happened again.
The nest's become a time machine
and for one aching moment
you're back.

Work in Progress

What do you need from me?
What notes should I take?
What corrections can I make
to my clothes, body, manner of speech?

I've been workshopped before,
complimented on my ability to
discard sentences without sentiment.
I discard pieces of myself the same way.

I take criticism and apply it,
welcome comments, concerns,
and complaints with a straight face.
Just tell me what you need.

Show me which unseemly bits to cut away,
where to pad my resume, point out where
I'm lacking, carve my essence into
something more efficient or effective.

Go line by line, trim the fat, incoherent
dialogue, failed fact-checked accusations,
pointless recitations.
You've heard it all before.

That's what I'm for, to be *proactive*;
recheck the data, put out the fires,
place the vase where the cat
won't realize how it shimmers.

Until it shatters.

Tomorrow I'll be better, arrive fresh eyed and
caffeinated with innovative ideas and solutions
as restitution for your time, your consideration
of my work—*of me*.

Body: A Lament

Not the boy-gazelle it was
in his pole-vaulting days, the beautiful
Italian girls at the side of the runway,
him sprinting past, planting, heels heavening
then downing, falling back like an
air-dropped angel into a few inches
of mill grit and cinders.

                    Not
the boy-trout who shivered upstream
through riffles at Third Bridge, cousin
to minnow and madtom.

                    Not
the boy-grub, wedging its scary way
into narrow cracks in Fox's Den cave,
then exhaling, just able to back out again
with the weight of sandstone Appalachia
pressing from all sides.

                    Not
the boy-serpent who could climb any tree
and loop itself and lounge there, eating
lunch from a back-pocket sack
in the blooming locust over the strip mine.

                    No.
Now, thicker, stout, tending to belly
and sag, (it seems more an *it*, lesser and lesser *him*)
hair thinning, spots on its hands
darkening maps of old age's counties,

but still game if not able for the heavy work of spade
and pitchfork and lugging, still
sweatable, legs and lungs, and
still getting, slowly, from here to there,

But no—that electric thing that
shocked itself stunned against a slow-dancing
fragrant girl, or juked and lost safeties on the field,
or grabbed, sure-handed, the sharp up-the-middle-single—

that almost weightless frame he could
fly in, or float through Latin class
like dreaming, or run for hours,
second-winding into trance and miles—no,

not the center anymore of a world of
fire and drink and freshness,
but worn now, used by nature for replacements,
continuation of the species, and soon to be

ditched, memories rifled,
pockets of the soul turned inside out,
just one letter of his name, a vowel, expiring in
breath gone breathless,

and now stooping, leaning against a trunk,
winded, among the pines he planted
as a boy, pines he would cut today, a few, just for
the proof of something—strength, joy, work, lasting—

But no, that body declares: *Not.*

Ordinary Time

The parochial vicar came into the kitchen at half past seven humming the opening bars to "How Great Thou Art" and smiling his open-faced, innocent-seeming smile. He raised the blinds above the sink and stopped to admire the sleek plumage of a cedar waxwing before exclaiming, "What a beautiful morning! Glory to God in the highest!"

Father James Dunn, the pastor of St. Mary's, took another drag on his cigarette and squinted through the haze at the young man. "Good morning Father Ryan," he said before returning to his black coffee and morning paper. "I'm glad to see you're feeling chipper."

"One-hundred percent," Father Ryan said with great enthusiasm. "Each day is a gift from God."

"Amen," Father Dunn said. "Though I don't think the McKenzies feel that way this morning."

He slid the obituaries over to Father Ryan, who scanned the page. The lead item was about a 32-year-old woman who had died of an overdose. The paper didn't say anything about that, of course, only that she'd been a loving mother to her two grade-school aged children and a promising artist who taught a popular course at the local community college.

But the truth about her death was there in the first paragraph for everyone to read. It was written in a code that had become all too plain for the members of Father Dunn's congregation. She had died suddenly, the obituary said, and the whole town knew what that meant.

"Such a tragedy," Father Ryan sighed, turning to grab a mug from the cabinet next to the sink. "Seems she was a beautiful young woman."

"Yes," Father Dunn said. "She was."

His voice caught and the younger priest turned to look at him.

Father Dunn took one last drag on his cigarette then stabbed it out on the ashtray. He drained the last of his coffee, got up and rinsed the mug in the sink. An antique cuckoo clock donated by a parishioner marked three quarters past the hour.

Crossing to the door, he told Father Ryan he would handle the 8 a.m. Mass. "You'd better head over to the McKenzies'," he said. "They'll be expecting someone to drop by."

Father Ryan nodded and resumed humming his favorite hymn as he fixed his coffee and looked for something sweet in the breadbox. Words Father Dunn left unsaid hung heavily in the air with the stale cigarette smoke.

Father Ryan opened a window. It was mid-June, six weeks after Easter. Ordinary Time.

What had been left unsaid was this: The McKenzie's are expecting someone to drop by and *I can't go*.

Why couldn't he go? That was something Father Dunn thought about as he donned his robes in the sacristy. That was something he thought about as he prepared the altar for Mass. That was something he thought about as he looked over his homily. "Why can't I go?" he asked himself.

It just wouldn't be right.

* * *

A year or two earlier, Father Dunn had been staying at a small secular residential treatment facility outside Berkeley Springs, West Virginia. On some mornings, he would sit by himself at one of the picnic tables to smoke a cigarette and admire the beauty of the hills.

It was on just such a morning that he'd first met her.

She'd approached him warily and asked to bum a cigarette. She had blonde hair dark at the roots and a wide-eyed, slightly terrified gaze. Her fingers were long and nervous and the nails were bitten down to the quick. She didn't know what to do with her hands. She tucked a length of hair behind her left ear and then pulled it out and tugged at it thoughtfully. She took a lighter out of her pocket and flicked it a few times before dropping it on the gravel path next to the picnic table.

Father Dunn reached over and picked it up and handed it back to her. When she fumbled with it again, he took it from her and stood awkwardly, his legs trapped by the picnic table, and lit her cigarette.

"I'm such a klutz," she said.

"It's no problem."

They stood there silently for a few moments before Father Dunn sat back down.

"Beautiful morning, isn't it," he said.

"Yeah," she said. "Not bad."

"I've been thinking about the movie *The Shining*. You know it?"

"Oh sure. We used to watch it sleepovers. You know, Halloween? Try to scare ourselves."

"Sure."

"That's an old movie."

"I guess it is. I keep thinking about the scene where Nicholson tries to sell his soul for a glass of beer. I've been thinking I know what that feels like now."

"Shit yeah," she said, blowing cigarette smoke out of the corner of her mouth. "But I gotta go with the harder stuff."

"Right," he said, nodding.

"Ain't no way I'm selling my soul for no goddamn glass a beer."

"Whiskey."

"Vodka."

"Single malt scotch."

"A gin and tonic."

"Now you're talking."

"You ever have a buttery nipple?" she said.

"No," Father Dunn said, coughing. "I don't think I have."

"Oh man, ya gotta try it. You take Bailey's Irish Cream and pour it over butterscotch schnapps. It's the best."

"Sounds delicious," he said, clearing his throat and taking another drag on his cigarette.

"It's the best," she said, smiling slightly.

"I'll have to try it sometime."

"You should."

They fell silent again, smoking and shivering in the early morning cold.

"I guess we shouldn't be talking like this, huh?" she said.

"It's okay," he said. "I won't tell if you won't."

"Okay. It'll be our little secret."

"Deal," he said. "I'm Jim."

"Ashley," she said. "McKenzie. Ashley McKenzie. That's my name."

"Jim Dunn."

"Nice to meet you Jim."

"Nice to meet you too."

* * *

Father Dunn smoked another cigarette and then returned to his room. It was warm inside, almost too warm, but it felt good after being out in the cold. There was still another half hour or so before breakfast so he took out the letter from the auxiliary bishop. It had arrived the day before in response to his most recent request for laicization. The bishop, who'd been one of his instructors at seminary, was trying to discourage him from leaving the priesthood.

The letter was written in the formal style of the church. It said that the bishop would not forward his request to the Vatican at this time because he could find no indication that Father Dunn had lost his faith or was otherwise incapable of fulfilling his mission as a priest. His current predicament was unfortunate but would ultimately serve as a test of both his faith and his courage. The bishop felt confident that Father Dunn would meet and conquer this challenge and emerge both as a stronger man and as a more devoted priest, ready to serve in whatever capacity the Lord may choose to use him.

A brief addendum to the letter gave Father Dunn some comfort. The bishop said he was praying for him daily and returned often to one of the papers he'd written for his class on the church in the world. It was on the Grand Inquisitor chapter of "The Brothers Karamazov" and the way the institutional church often inhibits the true mission of Christ. "You've always had a feel for that mission," the bishop wrote. "Keep that instinct and you will come through this trial all right."

After rereading the letter, Father Dunn decided to wait before submitting his next request.

* * *

The next day was a Sunday, laundry day. After rising early and saying Mass in his room, Father Dunn went down to put in a load of clothes. The building was quiet at this hour and he took out a novel to pass the time. It was a spy thriller he'd picked up from a pile of discarded books in the common room. He was just getting to the part where the main character entered the Kremlin in disguise when he heard footsteps outside the door.

"We've got to stop meeting like this," he said as Ashley came into the room.

"I think we're the only ones who get up this early," she said.

"Seems that way. What's your excuse?"

"Looking for the vending machines. They serve breakfast so late on Sundays."

"To save money, I guess. I try to think of it as brunch."

"What's brunch?"

"Breakfast and lunch? Brunch? You've never heard the term?"

"Not around here."

"Well, it's a big to-do in the city. I used to go to brunch almost every Sunday when I lived in New York."

"You lived in New York?"

"For a time. Graduate school after finishing seminary."

"Are you a priest?" she asked, giving him a sidelong glance as if trying to imagine him in a Roman collar instead of a ratty sweatshirt.

"Guilty as charged," he said, shrugging his shoulders.

"Far out," she said. "You don't seem like a priest."

"Thanks. I'll take that as a compliment."

"I mean, you just seem, like, normal."

Father Dunn laughed and shrugged his shoulders again. "I suppose I am, in my way," he said.

"I don't think I've ever been friends with a priest before. I'm not sure how I feel about it."

"Well, just take it one step at a time. Seems you're stuck with me for the moment anyway. Where else are you going to find such stimulating conversation so early in the morning?"

"Yeah," she said, her voice trailing off. "One step at a time. Works for me. Though I gotta tell you Father, I've got a bit of a potty-mouth."

"Perfectly all right with me."

"And I ain't exactly Mother Theresa."

"Hey, who is?"

"But I guess we can be friends, with those caveats."

"Okay," Father Dunn said.

"Great," Ashley said. She bounded over to the steel table where Father Dunn was sitting and hopped up next to him. He could smell the scent of her apple shampoo and feel the warmth of her body. Their shoulders were nearly touching. A small thrill went through his body and he tried to ignore it by fiddling with his book. He was trying to think of something to say when the buzzer on the washer went off and he jumped down to change the load.

"How long you been a priest?" she asked him.

"Almost ten years," he said.

"Really?"

"Yeah, but I'm trying to get out of it."

"Oh yeah? Is that hard to do?"

"Harder than you think."

"You can't just quit?"

"Not really."

"What happened? You lose your faith? Lotta times you see these guys on TV and they lose their faith. Or their wife died or something—not priests, I guess—and they want to leave the church or whatever. That happen to you?"

"Not exactly," he said. "It's just a lot of . . . internal politics. I wouldn't want to bore you with it."

"Nothing else to do around here."

"I suppose you're right. Some other time maybe."

"Fine by me. I never could stand church anyway."

"Why not?"

"It just always gave me the creeps. All that incense and chanting? It's not for me."

"Did you grow up Catholic?"

"My stepdad was real religious. He used to drag us to mass every Sunday. And I had to go to CCD—Catholic education for us public school heathens, you know?"

"I'm familiar with it. There are some good programs."

"Well, when you find one, let me know."

"That bad, huh?" he said, looking at her.

"Hated it," she said, staring ahead and stretching her legs out in front of her before letting them dangle again. "Waste of time."

"I'm sorry to hear that."

"It's alright. I learned a few things, I guess. Enough to know that it wasn't for me."

"I can understand that."

Father Dunn finished loading his whites into the dryer and his darks into the washer. He inserted the quarters for the machines and turned them both on. The room smelled like fabric softener and old paint. And beneath that the smell of Ashley's shampoo. He went back to sit on the table with her but made a point to leave some space between them. The room thrummed with the sound of the washer and dryer.

"Hey Father," Ashley said, scooting closer to him so she could be heard above the machines. "One thing I always wondered."

"What's that?"

"Why do they call it 'Ordinary Time.'"

"Ordinary Time?"

"Yeah. All the parts of the year that aren't Easter or Christmas or, whatever, feast days. Why do they call it that? You'd think they'd be able to come up with a better name."

"Yes, I suppose so."

"In a way, I like it though. It's like—ordinary time—just regular time. Good things can happen in ordinary time too. Just everyday time. Like this. Just sitting and talking."

"I see your point. I like that interpretation. Ordinary time."

"Is that why they call it that?"

"Well, no. It's actually Latin. It comes from the word 'ordinalis.' It just means the Sundays are numbered in a series. You know, like the second Sunday in Ordinary Time? Or the thirty fourth. Or what have you."

"That's it?"

"Yes, I'm sorry," Father Dunn said, chuckling. "I'm afraid the church isn't very imaginative when it comes to things like that."

"It's okay. I like my idea better though."

"Yes. Me too, actually."

Ashley glanced at the clock above the door.

"Shit," she said. "I'm supposed to meet my sponsor now."

"Okay," Father Dunn said. "See you at brunch?"

"See you," Ashley said, hopping down from the steel table and walking off toward the door.

Father Dunn tried to avoid watching her as she walked away. He said a quick prayer to himself and returned to his spy novel. Suddenly, the adventures of the main character didn't seem as interesting to him. When the buzzer went off, he nearly jumped out of his skin.

* * *

After meeting with her sponsor, Ashley went back to her room for a few minutes before brunch. While she was there, she happened to check her email and found a new message from her stepfather. After she had read it twice, she didn't feel much like eating. It was about her mother.

Dear Ashley, it began.

Your mother is going in for some tests this week. She has not been feeling well. We expect it might be breast cancer but we don't know for sure. They've made wonderful advances in treatment in recent years and I don't want you to worry too much.

Ashley inhaled sharply and continued reading.

I did want to take a moment to speak to you about some of your recent behavior. I hope you'll forgive me for saying this but some of your antics have put a lot of strain on your mother and I can't help but think we wouldn't be in this position if you'd just learn to control your impulses. You're a beautiful, spirited young woman but you take things too far sometimes.

Ashley laughed at that line. "Jesus," she thought. "Where does this guy come up with this stuff?"

Your mother and I would like to see you settle down a bit. You have children now and they need you. Lord knows we can't look after them forever. You need to take responsibility for your actions. That's what I've been trying to tell you. But you won't listen to me. Or anyone else for that matter. I'm sorry to go on like this but someone needs to say something.

The rage began to bubble up inside her. "Goddamn him," she thought. "After everything, he has the nerve to say this."

So you take the time you need to get cleaned up. Don't worry about us, though we will be worrying about you. Your momma will be fine. She's a strong woman. The Good Lord gave her a strong constitution. And your kids will be fine too. I'm looking after them. They love you but they're doing fine. Just do what you need to. No backsliding now. We're all counting on you. But you take care of yourself. We will take care of things here.

"Great, thanks, Bill," she thought. "Asshole."

Love,

Bill

P.S. I know you blame me for . . . something. I don't know what it is. I tried my best. I pray the Good Lord helps you to see that. We need you here.

Ashley balled up the letter, threw it in the trash can next to her desk and gave the can the finger.

* * *

A few days later, Ashley ran into Father Dunn in the hallway outside the common room. She asked him if he had a few minutes to talk and they ducked into the chapel. The place was spare, just a few benches and a raised platform at one end. There were some banners above the platform that said things like "Peace" and "Justice." An old lithograph of the prayer to St. Francis hung above the light switch.

"Where have you been?" Father Dunn asked. "I haven't seen you for a while."

"I haven't felt much like socializing," Ashley said.

"Something wrong?"

"My mom might be sick. She is sick, I think. I don't know. I got a letter from my stepfather."

"I'm so sorry."

"Will you pray for her, Father?"

"Of course."

"I don't get along too well with my family."

"I can understand that."

"But if anything ever happened to her . . ."

Ashley burst into tears and Father Dunn put his arms around her. He felt her body move against him. She looked up. There were tears in her bright green eyes. He leaned down to kiss her.

At that moment, there was a sound at the door.

"Excuse me," a big, no-nonsense woman named Esther said. She was Ashley's sponsor.

"Yes?" Father Dunn said, clearing his throat and standing up straight.

"It's time for my meeting with Ashley."

"Yes, of course."

Ashley pulled away from Father Dunn and dabbed at her eyes with the sleeves of her oversized Marshall University sweatshirt. Father Dunn squeezed her shoulders and, in a paternal display of affection, looked into her eyes and asked her if she was going to be okay.

"Yes," she said. "I'll be fine."

She sniffed a couple of times and wiped her eyes again. She gave him a little smile and walked off in the direction of her sponsor.

Esther watched her walk past her and down the hall. "Father," she said, nodding at him. And then she was gone too.

* * *

The following weekend, Ashley wandered into the common room early on a Sunday morning. Looking for something to do, she rifled through the pile of magazines and newspapers on one of the tables. There, in the middle of the pile, was a copy of *The New York Times*. On the front page, below the fold, was the beginning of a long story about the local diocese. It delineated a pattern of financial malfeasance and sexual abuse that was shocking in its detail. These things did not bother Ashley, who had taken a renewed interest in the business of the church. What bothered her was seeing Father Dunn's name in the article.

The accusations involved a defrocked ex-bishop and a series of young adults and minors who were seeking to become priests. According to the story, the bishop plied the young men with attention and alcohol, ultimately taking advantage of two of them. Father Dunn, who had been acting at the time as the bishop's secretary, was accused of not doing enough to stop the abuse, though the article noted he had twice tried to warn his superiors about the pattern. In the end, he had been relieved of his duties and sent into exile. His sin appeared to be one of omission rather than commission. This gave Ashley little comfort as she finished reading the article. To her it was more evidence that her trust had once again been misplaced.

She took the article from the common room, which was a violation of the center's rules, and carried it with her outside, where she expected to find Father Dunn smoking his first cigarette of the day after saying mass in his room. Sure enough, he was there.

"What the fuck is this?" Ashley said, tossing the paper on the picnic table.

Father Dunn looked at her and his heart sank. He picked up the paper gingerly, as if it were radioactive, and unfolded it. He read the first few paragraphs of the article and sighed.

"Ashley, I can explain," he started to say.

"Don't bother," she said. "You're a creep. Stay away from me."

She spat on the ground in front of him, turned and walked away. The word "creep" seemed to echo from the hills. The morning was cold and bright. Too bright. It began to give Father Dunn a headache.

* * *

Time went by. Eventually, Father Dunn completed his course of treatment and his time at the rehab center came to an end. One morning, toward the end of September, he was standing outside the center waiting for his ride. As always, he was smoking a cigarette. As it happened,

Ashley was outside that morning too, waiting for a ride to the hospital so she could visit her mother.

Father Dunn tried to ignore her gaze under the tall carport, but he found he couldn't. She came over to speak to him. He braced himself for another confrontation but none came. Instead, Ashley asked him if she could bum another cigarette. He took the pack out so fast it almost fell out of his hands and she laughed as he fumbled with his lighter.

"Here," she said, taking it from him and lighting her own cigarette. "I think I can manage now."

"That's good," he said, smiling as she handed him back his lighter.

"Heading out?" she said, touching his heavy black duffel bag with her toe.

"Yep," he said. "Back to the salt mines."

"That bad, huh?"

"No. Truth be told, I'm glad to be going back."

"Where are they sending you this time?"

He said the name of a town. A look of recognition passed over her face.

"Hey!" she said. "That's my town."

"Good," he said. "I'll be close by if you need me."

"We just might. I'm heading to the hospital now to see my mom."

"How's she doing?"

"Okay, so far. But it doesn't look good."

"I'm sorry."

"It's okay."

"I'll pray for her."

"Thank you."

An awkward silence followed. It reminded Father Dunn of when they'd first met. He wished he could go back to that moment. He wished he could go back to the beginning of time. He saw a car in the distance.

"Looks like my ride's here," he said, finishing his cigarette and gathering up his bags.

Ashley just nodded.

"Well, I guess I'll be seeing you," he said as the car pulled up.

"Father," Ashley said, reaching for his arm. "Wait."

He stopped in his tracks.

"I'm sorry about what I said. You're not a creep."

"It's okay," he said, waving away her concerns. "We don't need to get into it."

"No," Ashley said. "I'm sorry, really. You're a good man."

"Am I?" Father Dunn said, starting to choke up. "How do you know?"

"I just know."

"I tried to do the right thing," he said, his voice faltering. "I wrote letters. I . . ."

"I know."

"It wasn't enough. I should have done more."

"I understand."

"I'm sorry!" he cried out, sobbing now. She embraced him. They stood there like that for several minutes. The young priest driving the car drummed his fingers on the steering wheel and hummed the first few bars of "How Great Thou Art."

Eventually, Father Dunn composed himself. "I'm sorry," he said again. "I didn't mean to lose control of my emotions like that."

"It's okay," Ashley said. "It's a good thing, I think."

"And I'm sorry about everything else. Everything."

"It's okay. You're forgiven."

Father Dunn smiled and laughed. "Thank you," he said. "I guess I'd better be going."

"See you around," Ashley said.

* * *

Father Dunn thought of all this as he was saying Mass and after, as he undressed in the sacristy. He looked out the window and saw a yellow mop bucket and a broom and, halfway up the hill beyond, a deer and two fawns traversing the greenery. He looked away and when he turned back they were gone. He went into the rectory.

He had been unable to visit the McKenzies when Ashley's mother died. He'd been on a retreat out west and anyway it was probably for the best. He'd avoided the whole family when he'd gotten to town and lost touch with Ashley. Last he'd heard she'd been down in Florida somewhere, getting her life back together.

Maybe it had worked for a while. Sometimes it did.

On the table in the kitchen were some letters, including one from the Vatican. It was in a cream-colored envelope with an impressive dark script on the outside. On the inside was a short letter informing him that the Holy Father had seen fit to grant his request for laicization. There would be a small payment sent to him to help with resettlement. There was no note wishing him well. He was being cashiered out.

He looked at the antique clock above the sink. It was a terribly ugly thing. Dark shingles dripped down a steeply gabled roof above a faded stucco façade out of which a beak-less and eyeless bird appeared every hour to mark the time. It ticked loudly, ominously, each stroke of the second hand a blow to the air. *Tick-tock. Tick-tock. Tick-tock.* The sound boomed in the closed space. Ordinary time.

Jim Dunn dropped the letter. It fell a great distance to the linoleum floor. He listened to the clock beat the air until it made him sick. Then he walked out of the kitchen. He would see the McKenzies. He would give them whatever comfort he could. He would set things right. He would do everything right, this time.

Where I Was When the World Was Ending

I raced toward the punchline of a cruel joke.
After five years in the pen, I earned parole,
made it out to a home not my home, &
I had one week to build a life & enjoy it
before an asteroid hit, the sun exploded,
or the Great Contraction un-Banged the universe,
some disaster according to the Mayans,
according to myth & interpretations of myth,
street preachers shouting gospels not their own.
Everyone feared we were going to die,
although no one believed it. I kept an open mind.
I expected it to be my luck to breathe free air
as it turned to ash, imprisoning me in darkness.
I tried to make myself comfortable
amidst boxes dropped off by my ex.
I ate everything I could touch—
pancakes & pizzas, candy bars & cakes—&
called this pleasure, called it delight.
I'd pass fatter if I had to go,
so bloated when bombs exploded
or the world-tree burned, my consciousness
could survive an extra half a second
outside walls & razor-wire fences,
where I hadn't finished unpacking
as the hour of prophecy arrived.

The Dinosaurs of the Mid-Atlantic

The dinosaurs of Pennsylvania,
Maryland, and West Virginia
show themselves in winter mainly.
They slide down snowy slopes
in Poconos and Alleghenies.
They do not see, nor
do they hear, the meteor.
But they can feel it in their bones.

Christmas 1964, Martins Ferry, Ohio

In old St Mary's Church,
In the minutes before the midnight bells,
I contemplate families like mine.
Polacks and Slovaks and other assorted Bohunks,
Resplendent, rejoicing, reverent.

And my knuckle-scarred father,
Whispering a blessing
On his hard dirty job
With everyday heroes
Insuring the dreams of their children.

And his well-loved wife,
Arranging her little and middle and fledgling chicks
On an oaken bench
Burnished by generations of prudent cotton and gabardine.

So, I murmur my own thanksgiving,
For this family,
And our clear autumn evenings
Away from Friday night lights.
Directing my father's handcrafted spyglass
To the future and the splendors of the Universe.

Sonnet for the Builders

Stacked brickwork steadies the sides of an abandoned building,
as reliable as the men who smoothed the mortar, laid the brick
and tamped each one with the turned-down handle of his trowel.

Sunset illuminates the windows of the old factory, a warm glow
belying the cold silence that reigns where machines once hummed
and workers bustled, hope for a bright future lighting their eyes

like the wide eyes of our nation's children turned to their teachers
in other buildings across the land. Those who do the work of builders
lay down facts and ideas, smoothing the way for ardent dreamers

who will outlive them. Behind rows of windows, open to fresh
breath and clear light of knowledge, sit the young, alive as flames
and eager to build a future only they can imagine. Let them hold fast

to these days, gain courage from their forebears, lest the pain
of closed opportunities, like closed factories, put out the lights.

Pittsburgh: A Portrait

3J—
the bull's eye:
skirted for acres all directions around
the rectangular immensity of downtown
by salt-bitter ground
by crisscrossed sirens
snow-searchlights
a point of impact
from helicopters down
from trucks beaming up
hard white bars
sweep the orange glow
of dim Pittsburgh's skyline
and the faces like snow
like soot of people
snoring under the opaque solemn faces
of each building:
Fifth Avenue Place
tan state-tinted angles
haughty gothic PPG
five friends' crown-tips spearing
Egypt-gold and pyramidic Gulf Tower
the people climbing
Oxford squatting
K & L Gates roomy
Highmark unaffable
BNY Mellon Center
whose corporate name resigns
sacred weight

stone bears down:
people gaze from Fifth and Grant
work drink fight drink smoke
work drink game gamble
work smoke game work
under each building
those already catalogued
those slanting and emptied
those condemned those burned
those demolished those rented
those that house stale coal
those that are mortar middens
the unnamed buildings of overdriven Pittsburgh
the rooms where the city plots
where bonnie Carnegie filled honeypots
the zones of rare birds
the mills boiling sand into glass
the hard ones in clouds
the hard ones under trees
the ones that were musket shades
the crests that fret over barges
the gin-filled tugboat cabins
the droopy bins of aspirin
the ones where belts convey Pittsburgh
to structures of stern brick
and blasted wet wood
the nethermost cells of Fort Pitt
the grapeshot's blind post
the cash-counting houses
cooled by Clay Frick's ghost

and finally like the colossus:
U.S. Steel Tower of 1970
seeming to lean against the diagonal snowfall

absorbed in moody sky
takes Pittsburgh on its back
the people climbing
up rusted sides lit forever
in 1920s amber
cool plum brown gray purple
glaring between rich hills on all sides
a density of steel
of capital letters
brilliantly crowding
the rivers

the rivers ancient and triple:
one courses katabatic passages beneath the city
two others surf limestone down the valley
crashing together
the reordered rivers
rich with French blood
into muddy Mon' phase Al's bubbles
as they press against new chemistry
Allegheny:
what are you fixing to do
raise turtle whirls high
trip southward like a canoe
Monongahela: halt
linger
repel Al's fish
die in the Ohio
be brilliant
hurry to Kentucky

The Flying Squirrels

Strange, nocturnal sounds—
frozen January, time to fill
the feeders. Opening the shed door,

something—a chipmunk?—darting
from wall to wall, spreading out
what looked like bat wings,

staring back at me
with huge bug eyes as if
I was the intruder.

I slammed the door once, twice,
in hopes to scare it back out,
but no, it's happy with this shelter

and the plastic bag of birdseed
it ripped open and scattered across
the green tarp lining the wooden floor.

I considered the diminishing
number of cardinals, woodpeckers,
mourning doves pecking

not so patiently at the white ground,
waiting for their order to arrive.
Opening the door again, slowly, stepping back,

peeking into the dark cavern—
in the far corner, a small bowl of shredded bark
and dry leaves, balanced on the hemlock board,

the tan furry thing beside it—
and another of the same kind flung out
and I flung back, thinking rabies,

and—who knows?—typhus,
rodents swarming in my sleep.
Didn't I read, once: *endangered,*

a priority species, protected—
prefers old growth forests, conifers?
They cluster to keep warm.

What about the live trap,
fill it with seed? Haul them,
one at a time, into the woods where

they can carry on their love affair
and dreams for the future
and we could lure back

our multi-colored birds,
reseal the cracks in the shed?
This morning, checking

the trap, locked in—curled up—which one?—
in the corner of the cage—
innocuous, a child's toy, eyes open.

Buried it in the woods.
Laid branches over its tiny body.
Returned the trap back to the barn.

Thought about the other.
Gliding like a ghost.

The Silver Aesthetics of Winter Rain

Iced world tangle
of pearly frozen branches.

Each encased limb an ancient radio
of a frozen world.

Clear vacuum tubes of fractal filaments
transmit crackling song.

The Silent Season

Arctic air and our journey through January begins.
Doors and windows open wide today,
blow out all ill and evil of the past year.

We dig into hilled fruits and vegetables,
buried in October against freeze,
thrill with energy of red and yellow apples,
the delicacy of fresh cabbage.

November rain lies frozen
on cliffs and rocks,
in thick rivers of ice.
We watch light reflected there,
wait for water drip, move again.

Our elders forget this ground is frozen,
lie down to rest and do not get up.
This month we howl at Wolf Moon,
and into every hole the dead leave in our lives.

Now is the center of winter,
in white and gray of morning sky
we look back and lean forward,
toss corn and tobacco into frigid air.

In this silent season we learn,
in a flicker of heat,
that for most of our world,
the meaning of life is simply,
a glint of warmth and something to eat.

Full Moon

As I back out of the garage and pull the car toward the woods I see her, shining full circle, white as alabaster behind the bare trees that stand like soldiers guarding her, the top branches spidery against the moonlit sky. She lights up their silhouette.

I put the car in drive and look forward through more trees stripped of their greenery like a storefront mannequin stripped of its clothes, seeming to shiver in the bitter cold, fencing the yard. Beyond them is an unusual beginning to sunrise—on the horizon before me, over the mountain ridges, horizontal lines of blues, purples and grays layer like a cake. The color is so different from what is normal at this time of day in mid-winter. So often the tips of the trees in our yard seem to stand like little candles above the mountain ridge iced with colors of orange and pink and red—a mingling of color that I cannot identify. But the colors on this morning do not exude such fiery energy; they are colors of cool and calm, the product of the full moon in a clear sky.

The morning is still as I pass down our steep driveway and into the neighborhood. Some crunchy ice lines the road, snow coats the grass, everything looks black and white as a checkerboard.

As I pull onto the freeway, she greets me with a force that makes me want to stop the car. The moon is so bright—white with a yellow halo— that her craters are fully visible. She lights up a midnight blue sky. There are no other cars on the road. Just me and the moon. As I drive toward Brownsville and the Historic Church of St. Peter, where I play the organ, the sky lightens to ocean blue, and the moon continues to command the scene before me. When I get to my exit, I do not want to leave her. Today the sun will eat away the snow. The ground will be raw and black. The moon will start to lose her full luster.

At the church I park "outside the lines" on the pavement, unable to see well in the morning dusk. As I make my way down the hill, I look over the cemetery that flanks the church; graves of Revolutionary and Civil War soldiers sit amidst the grander tombstones of priests and wealthy parishioners. As I make my way toward the church, I get one last glimpse of the moon sitting beside the green copper Gothic steeple. The church sits high on a hill overlooking Brownsville, the Monongahela River and Route 40; it is believed that the Catholic Irish immigrants who built St. Peter's wanted their church to sit above the many others in the town, wanted it to be seen from every angle entering Brownsville. I stand in the parking lot and look. The only other person there is an usher. "It's beautiful isn't it," he says in a hushed voice. There are no cars on Route 40. Stillness blankets the earth.

I shiver in the tomblike cold of the old stone church as I climb the narrow stone turret to the organ and choir loft. Before Mass begins, I play hymns about light because that is the theme of the gospel—salt and the light that pierced the darkness.

I often find myself stuck in the gap between black of night and the hallelujah of a sunrise. Don't we all get stuck there, unsure if we should remain hidden in the shadows of the night or embrace the light that is beckoning to us. Our hope hides behind the haze. We keep checking the sky, anticipating that at some point the clouds will clear. But sometimes the epiphany of purpose we seek remains clouded. Sometimes we shrink into that gap between dark and light because it is safe there. We don't have to go back to the things that hurt us, and we don't have to move forward, afraid that our flaws, our failures will be glaringly obvious in the sunlight. I lack the courage to take risks, generally allowing myself to rest in the shadows. I have sought purpose for a long time, not understood what was meant for me. I have traveled the road back and forth, back and forth, again and again seeking what gift I had to give this place, this landscape that was defined by revolutionists and immigrants.

The moon in her brilliance beckons me to allow a beam to break the night of my heart. She reminds me that our repetitive passage over the road can only be made sure by the places that we stop along it, that I need to spend less time thinking about what I am doing here and more time thinking about how I can serve here? How can I be a part of the landscape rather than just moving back and forth on it? How can I stop in the road to view the moons of my life, the sites that must be seen now before they disappear?

This moon that I see on this February morning is a Snow moon. It isn't as brilliant as the Wolf Moon, the first full moon of 2023 which appeared on January 6, my 58th birthday. Astrologists say these moons named for howling wolves and drifting snows are supposed to cause me deep reflection and an unfiltered view of myself, that a purple sky signifies a spiritual awakening. In the Bible and in many churches, purple represents royalty, priesthood and wealth. We look for signs—full moons, purple skies, other things in nature that really have nothing at all to do with our lives and our decisions. We look for road signs to guide us, mile markers to help us to see the length until the end.

My journey to find myself, to reclaim the person who seems to have receded in the shadows of a moonless sky, has been one of exterior exploration and interior roadwork. I have looked back on the roads of southwestern Pennsylvania where I have lived my entire life for grounding and guidance, and I have looked forward for possible routes of escape. What I have found is a permanent mapping that will always ground me.

CONTRIBUTOR BIOS

Roy Bentley

Roy Bentley is the author of *Walking with Eve in the Loved City*, chosen by Billy Collins as finalist for the Miller Williams poetry prize; *Starlight Taxi*, winner of the Blue Lynx Poetry Prize; *The Trouble with a Short Horse in Montana*, chosen by John Gallaher as winner of the White Pine Poetry Prize; as well as *My Mother's Red Ford: New & Selected Poems 1986–2020* published by Lost Horse. Work has appeared in *The Louisville Review*, *december*, *Crazyhorse*, *The Southern Review*, *Rattle*, *Shenandoah*, and *Prairie Schooner* among others. His latest book of poems is *Beautiful Plenty* (Main Street Rag, 2021).

David Blackmore

David Blackmore grew up first in Pittsburgh and later in Kane, Pennsylvania. After many years of teaching at New Jersey City University, he is now an associate professor of English and the Writing Program Coordinator at Chatham University in Pittsburgh. David has published in *Rockvale Review*, *Wordrunners eChapbooks*, *Watershed Journal*, and *Allium*, and he recently completed his memoir manuscript *Chemical Works Road*.

Aidan Bobik

Aidan Bobik (he/him) is an undergraduate student at Chatham University where he studies political science and history. He is proudly from St. Marys, Pennsylvania—a fact he could talk for hours about—and enjoys a good walk.

Ace Boggess

Ace Boggess is author of six books of poetry, most recently *Escape Envy* (Brick Road Poetry Press, 2021). His writing has appeared in *Michigan*

Quarterly Review, Notre Dame Review, Harvard Review, and other journals. An ex-con, he lives in Charleston, West Virginia, where he writes and tries to stay out of trouble. His seventh collection, *Tell Us How to Live,* is forthcoming in 2024 from Fernwood Press.

Maggie Burnette

Maggie Burnette is an up-and-coming poet in the Appalachia region. Maggie enjoys writing about their upbringing of being an Appalachian in Baltimore, their Appalachian family background, and still living in Appalachia as a queer Jew by choice. They currently live in Morgantown with their husband and two cats Kiwi and Ted.

Beth Casteel

Beth Casteel is a candidate for the MFA in Creative Nonfiction at Carlow University. She is writing about life along the National Road Heritage Corridor and lives in rural southwestern Pennsylvania.

Greg Clary

Greg Clary is a retired college professor who was born and raised in Turkey Creek, West Virginia, and now resides in the northern Appalachia Pennsylvania Wilds. His photographs have been published in *The Sun Magazine, Looking at Appalachia, Rattle, Hole in the Head Review, Tiny Seed Literary Journal, The Watershed Journal, About Place, Dark Horse, Change Seven, Detour Ahead, Bee House Journal, Appalachian Lit, North/South Appalachia, The Ear, Bluestone Review, Stick Figure Poetry, Rubbertop Journal,* and many other publications. His writing and poems have appeared in *The Rye Whiskey Review, The Bridge Literary Arts Journal, Pine Mountain Sand & Gravel, Northern Appalachia Review, Pittsburgh Post-Gazette, Waccamaw Journal, Rusty Truck, Anti-Heroin Chic, Sterling Clack Clack, Trailer Park Quarterly, Tobeco, Clinch, Off the Coast Magazine, Rust Belt Review, Unlimited Literature, Black Shamrock,* and *North/South Appalachia: Poetry and Art, vols I & II.*

Michael Comiskey

Michael Comiskey is a retired professor of political science and economics at the Penn State Fayette Campus near Uniontown in Fayette County, Pennsylvania. He began writing poems—mostly formal—about his native region of northern Appalachia at age fifty. He lives in his hometown of Connellsville, Pennsylvania with his wife Mary Ann.

Bob Craven

Bob Craven is a poet, musician, and teacher born in Ellwood City, Pennsylvania. He studies working-class Appalachian culture from environmental and historical perspectives. He wrote the dissertation *Appalachian Moderns: Poetry and Music, 1936-1947* (2022) and the article "Documenting the Corporate Underworld in Mark Nowak's Coal Mountain Elementary" (2020). He teaches at Westminster College (New Wilmington, Pennsylvania) as an Assistant Professor.

M. C. Benner Dixon

M. C. Benner Dixon lives, writes, and grows things in Pittsburgh, Pennsylvania. She is quick to make a pun and slow to cut her grass. Her forthcoming books include *The Height of Land* (2022 Orison Fiction Prize winner) and *Millions of Suns* (with Sharon Fagan McDermott). Her poetry and fiction have appeared in *Reckoning*, *The Hopper*, *Appalachian Review*, and elsewhere.

Tom Donlon

Tom Donlon earned an MFA from American University in Washington, DC before moving to West Virginia in 1986. He was awarded a chapbook, *Peregrine*, in 2016 by the Franciscan University in Ohio. A full collection, *Apart, I Am Together*, was published in 2023 by Wipf and Stock. Recognition: Pushcart Prize nominations and a fellowship from the West Virginia Commission on the Arts.

Charlene Fix

Charlene Fix's poetry: *Taking a Walk in My Animal Hat* (Bottom Dog 2018), *Frankenstein's Flowers* (CW Books 2014), *Flowering Bruno* (XOXOX 2006), and *Jewgirl* (Broadstone, fall 2023), and prose: *Harpo Marx as Trickster* (McFarland 2013). Emeritus, Columbus College of Art and Design, she co-coordinates Hospital Poets at OSU hospitals, works for peace and justice, and is mother of three, grandmother of two. Her website: Charlenefix.com

Daniel Flatley

Daniel Flatley grew up in Wheeling, West Virginia, and lives near Washington, DC, with his family. His journalism has appeared in *Bloomberg News*, *Time* magazine and the *Washington Post*. His fiction and poetry have appeared in the *Northern Appalachia Review*.

Jane Ellen Freeman

Jane Ellen Freeman is a former language arts teacher and lives south of Shepherdstown, West Virginia. Jane has several published short stories in *Florida Writers Anthologies* as well as stories in *The Ghosts of Shepherdstown Vol. I* and forthcoming Vol. II. Other publications: *Beyond the Stone Eagle Gate* (YA), *The Whispering Chimney* (MG), and two others. Website: www.janeellenfreeman.com

John Grau

John Grau is a retired journalist and a member of the Stiller Nation in Delaware. His poems have appeared in regional anthologies in New York and Delaware. He is a contributor to the online blog *Sense of Decency* (senseofdecency.com), and at work on a memoir, *Diary of a Resurrected Man*.

Richard Hague

Richard Hague is a native of Steubenville, Ohio, and author or editor of 22 volumes, most recently, *Continued Cases* (Dos Madres Press 2023), poems satirical, political, ecological, and social. He was 1985 Co-Poet of the Year in Ohio, winner of the 2003 Appalachian Poetry Book of the Year, and the 2013 Weatherford Award in Poetry.

Lisa Harris

Lisa Harris is from the Allegheny Mountains; some of her Scottish ancestors walked from the Port of Philadelphia to settle there. Her publications include: 'Geechee Girls, Allegheny Dream, The Raven's Trail, (Ravenna Press), Traveling Through Glass, Dwelling Space (Cayuga Lake Books), Broken Open, Carry Light, Carry Fire (Wasteland Press). She lives in the Finger Lakes with her husband, Jeff Spence.

Amanda Hayden

Amanda Hayden, Poet Laureate and Humanities Professor, has received the League for Innovation Teaching Excellence award. Her chapter, "Saunter Like Muir," was published in Eco pedagogies, and her poems are published in several reviews and journals. She lives on a farm with her family with goats, pigs, chickens, and a duck named Dorothy.

Mary Pat Hyland

Mary Pat Hyland is a novelist/short story writer from Endwell, New York. Her works are set in the Southern Tier and Finger Lakes regions of New York state. Hyland, a graduate of Syracuse University and an award-winning former newspaper journalist, was selected as an Arts Center of Yates County Artist in Residence in 2013.

Kirk Judd

Kirk Judd has lived, worked, trout fished and wandered around in West Virginia all of his life. Kirk was a member of the Appalachian Literary League, a founding member and former president of West Virginia Writers, Inc. and is a founding member and creative writing instructor for Allegheny Echoes, Inc.

Hannah Allman Kennedy

Hannah Allman Kennedy is a writer and artist from the oil ghost towns of Venango County, Pennsylvania. Her debut novel, *And It All Came Tumbling Down*, was published in 2021 from the Watershed Journal Literary Group and was awarded Book of the Year at the 2023 WCoNA Writers Conference of Northern Appalachia®.

Jack Kogut

Jack Kogut, a native of Martins Ferry, Ohio, is a mostly amateur writer of mostly fiction. His work has recently appeared in *Northern Appalachia Review Volume 4* and *Phantom Kangaroo Issue 27* and not so recently in *The Washington Post* and *Omni Magazine*. He is a retired scientist and lives with his family in Maryland.

Martin Malone

Martin Malone's poems have appeared in Pennsylvania Bards Against Hunger 2018, the Pennsylvania Poetry Society 2021 Anthology, and a number of little magazines, including *Dream International Quarterly*, *Scribble*, *Seminary Ridge Review*, *Backbone Mountain Review* (winner of the 2022 BMR Poetry Prize), *CentraLit*, and the *Maryland Literary Review*. His chapbook, *Simple Gifts*, was published in 2014. He is one of the organizers of Gettysburg's First Friday Poetry Series. He lives in Gettysburg, Pennsylvania.

John C. Mannone

John C. Mannone has work in *Anthology of Appalachian Writers XV* [Barbara Kingsolver], *North Dakota Quarterly*, *Poetry South*, and *Baltimore Review*. He was awarded a Jean Ritchie Fellowship (2017). His newest collections are *Sacred Flute* (Iris Press) and *Song of the Mountains* (Middle Creek Publishing). He's an invited Professor of Creative Writing/Poetry at Alice Lloyd College in Kentucky.

Elizabeth McConnell

Elizabeth McConnell earned a BA in English from Hollins University, Roanoke, Virginia. She currently works for the Davis College of Agriculture, Natural Resources and Design at West Virginia University. Previously she has worked at the Morgantown Public Library in Morgantown, West Virginia and served on the Morgantown Public Library Board of Trustees. Elizabeth is an active member of the Morgantown Writers Group, Monongahela Master Naturalists, and West Virginia Writers, Inc.

Dennis McFadden

Dennis McFadden, a retired project manager, lives and writes in a cedar-shingled cottage called Summerhill in the woods of upstate New York. His collection, *Jimtown Road*, won the 2016 Press 53 Award for Short Fiction; his novel, *Old Grimes Is Dead*, was a Kirkus Reviews Best Indie Book of 2022. He has been previously published in *Northern Appalachia Review*.

Wendy McVicker

Wendy McVicker is the recent past poet laureate of Athens, Ohio, and a longtime teaching artist. Her most recent chapbook is *Zero, a Door* (The Orchard Street Press, 2021). She loves collaborations with writers and artists in other media. When she gets the chance, she performs with instrumentalist Emily Prince, under the name "another language altogether."

Martha Gallagher Michael

Martha Gallagher Michael is a Professor Emerita of education at Capital University, and professional artist. She exhibits locally and regionally; and has published poetry with *Pudding Magazine: Journal of Applied Poetry, Northern Appalachia Review* and at *Steinbecknow.com*. She also has two artworks as covers for *Pudding Magazine: Journal of Applied Poetry*.

Abby Minor

Abby Minor lives in the ridges and valleys of central Pennsylvania, where she works on poems, essays, gardens, and projects exploring regional & reproductive politics. Her first book, *As I Said: A Dissent* (Ricochet Editions, 2022), is a collection of long documentary poems concerning abortion, embodiment, justice, and citizenship in U.S. history.

Karen Whittington Nelson

Karen Whittington Nelson writes poetry and fiction from her home on a small Southeastern Ohio farm. Her work has been published by *Pine Mountain Sand & Gravel*, *Sheila-Na-Gig Online*, *I Thought I Heard a Cardinal Sing: Ohio's Appalachian Voices*, *Anthology of Appalachian Writers*, *Women Speak*, *Northern Appalachia Review*, *Gyroscope Review*, *Main Street Rag*, and other journals.

Joshua Penrod

Joshua Penrod works for an international trade association based in Washington, DC, though he resides in Bedford County, Pennsylvania. He has published books on commercial neuroscience and industrial history and has published several essays and peer-reviewed articles, including previous work in *The Loyalhanna Review* and the *Northern Appalachia Review*.

Sherry Poff

Sherry Poff grew up in West Virginia. She now lives and writes in and around Chattanooga, Tennessee. Sherry holds an MA in Writing from the University of Tennessee at Chattanooga and is a member of the Chattanooga Writers' Guild. Her work has appeared in numerous online and print publications including *Artemis*, *Anthology of Appalachian Writers*, and *Stone Poetry Quarterly*.

David B. Prather

David B. Prather is the author of *We Were Birds* (Main Street Rag Publishing, 2019), and his collection, *Bending Light with Bare Hands*, will be published by Fernwood Press. His work has appeared in many publications, including *Prairie Schooner*, *Cutleaf*, *OPEN: Journal of Arts & Letters*, *Sheila-Na-Gig*, and others. He has worked as an English professor and as an editor, and he is currently a reader for *Suburbia Journal*.

Bonnie Proudfoot

Bonnie Proudfoot's fiction, poetry, and essays have appeared in journals and anthologies. Her debut novel, *Goshen Road*, was selected the 2022 WCONA Book of the Year and long-listed for the 2021 PEN/Hemingway Award. Her first poetry chapbook, *Household Gods*, was published in September of 2022 by Sheila-Na-Gig Editions. She lives in Athens, Ohio.

Jaclyn Reed

Jaclyn Reed received her MFA in Writing from Carlow University and her BA in English from the University of Pittsburgh. Her work has appeared in *Adelaide*, *Northern Appalachia Review*, *The Sunlight Press*, and *Prime Number Magazine*, among others. She works in e-commerce solutions and lives across the way from Hershey's Reese's factory.

Alice Reynolds

Alice Reynolds lives in southern Ohio. She serves on the board of the Pump House Center for the Arts and volunteers there. She is also a member of the Southern Ohio Writers Collaborative. In addition to creative writing, Alice writes grants for the Pump House. Her creative work has appeared in the *Northern Appalachia Review* and online SOWC anthologies.

Amy Le Ann Richardson

Amy Le Ann Richardson was born and raised in Morehead, Kentucky, and holds an MFA from Spalding University ('09). Amy is a farmer, writer, visual artist, and teacher. She is the author of *Who You Grow Into*, Finishing Line Press, 2024. She lives and works on her farm in Carter County, Kentucky.

Chuck Salmons

Chuck Salmons is a poet and has served as part of the leadership for the Ohio Poetry Association for more than a decade. His poems have appeared in numerous journals and anthologies, including *Pudding Magazine*, *The Fib Review*, *Evening Street Review*, *The Ekphrastic Review*, and *Poets to Come: A Poetry Anthology* in celebration of Walt Whitman's Bicentennial. He has published two chapbooks, *Stargazer Suite* and *Patch Job*. Chuck is recipient of a 2018 Ohio Arts Council Individual Excellence Award for poetry, and he performs with the poetry trio Concrete Wink. chucksalmons.com

Maxim D. Shrayer

Maxim D. Shrayer is a bilingual author and a professor at Boston College. He was born in Moscow and emigrated in 1987. His recent books include *A Russian Immigrant: Three Novellas* and *Immigrant Baggage*, a memoir. Shrayer's new collection of poetry, *Kinship*, is forthcoming from Finishing Line Press.

Larry Smith

Larry Smith is a poet, fiction and memoir writer, as well as a literary biographer. He edits Bottom Dog Press and directs its Appalachian Writing Series.

Bill Smoot

Bill Smoot grew up in the Ohio River town of Maysville, Kentucky. He received a BA in philosophy at Purdue and a PhD in philosophy at Northwestern. He has published fiction and non-fiction in such periodicals as *Ninth Letter*, *Orchid*, *Crab Orchard Review*, *Barely South Review*, *Narrative*, *The Nation*, *Georgia Review*, and *Literary Review*. He has published a non-fiction book, *Conversations with Great Teachers*. He lives in Berkeley, California, with his dog Artemis and teaches college courses at San Quentin Prison.

Lois Spencer

Lois has taught English at Fort Frye High School, at Washington State Community College and Ohio Valley University, and in the ILR program at Marietta College. Publication credits include *Women's Speak*, *Anthology of Appalachian Writers*, *Persimmon Tree*, *The Poorhouse Rag*, *Change Seven*, as well as the *Northern Appalachia Review*. Her memoir, *In the Language of My Country*, highlights life in Southeastern Ohio.

Wayne Swanger

Wayne Swanger, a native of Pennsylvania, has published in *Friends Journal*, *The Watershed Journal*, *Tobeco*, *North/South Appalachia*, and *The Bridge Literary Arts Journal*. His poems have been shared via *Poets Against Racism and Hate* readings/website. His book, *Fields of His Heart*, was published by The Watershed Journal Literary Group (2020).

David M. Sweet

David M. Sweet, a retired high school English teacher and theater director, is a life-long resident of Southeastern Kentucky. A Berea College graduate with a background in journalism and public relations, his short story "Southbound" won a *reedsy.com* short story contest in October 2022. His writing centers around his life experiences, family history, and characters rooted in the region.

Philip Terman

Philip Terman's most recent books are *This Crazy Devotion* (Broadstone, 2020), *Our Portion: New and Selected Poems* (Autumn House, 2015) and, as co-translator, *Tango Beneath a Narrow Ceiling: The Selected Poems of Riad Saleh Hussein* (Bitter Oleander, 2021). A retired professor of English at Clarion University, he directs The Bridge Literary Arts Center in Franklin, Pennsylvania.

Matthew Ussia

Matthew Ussia is a professor, editor, podcaster, thereminist, writer, soft-core punk, social media burnout, and all-around sentient organic matter.

His first book of poetry, *The Red Glass Cat*, was published in 2021. His writings have appeared in *Mister Rogers and Philosophy*, *Trailer Park Quarterly*, and *Anti-Heroin Chic*, among others. He lives in Pittsburgh. More info can be found at matthewussia.com.

Dick Westheimer

Dick Westheimer lives in rural southwest Ohio. He is a *Rattle Poetry* Prize finalist. His poems have recently appeared in *Whale Road Review*, *Innisfree Journal*, *Gyroscope Review*, *Banyan Review*, *Rattle*, *Ritual Well*, *One Art* and *Cutthroat*. His chapbook, *A Sword in Both Hands, Poems Responding to Russia's War on Ukraine*, is published by *Sheila-Na-Gig*. More at www.dickwestheimer.com

Sherrell Wigal

Sherrell Wigal was born, raised and still lives in West Virginia. She writes from her rock-based road roots, with an eye and ear to women and a heart honed to the spirituality in life. To read Sherrell's poetry is to walk into a place we cannot always predict but is also somehow familiar. Her poems have appeared in many regional publications.

Linda Mills Woolsey

Linda Mills Woolsey grew up in Lawrence County, Pennsylvania and currently divides her time between Allegany County, New York and a place on French Creek in Crawford County, Pennsylvania. She's a retired college professor whose poems have appeared in *The Sow's Ear Poetry Review*, *Coal Hill Review*, *The Windhover*, *St. Katherine Review*, and other journals.

Kathryn Yelinek

Kathryn Yelinek lives in northeastern Pennsylvania, where she works as a librarian. Her work has appeared in *Deep Magic*, *Metaphorosis*, *Andromeda Spaceways Magazine*, and *Beneath Ceaseless Skies*. She has a fondness for retold fairy tales, hopepunk, and happily ever after. When her nose isn't buried in a book, she's frequently found talking to birds or gazing at the stars.

www.ingramcontent.com/pod-product-compliance
Lightning Source LLC
Chambersburg PA
CBHW011352010726
47494CB00008B/2287